God Bless! ♡

The Fall

The Fall

Based on a True Story

Todd James Myers

Seraph Books

www.seraphbooks.com

The Fall

Cover Design By: Alyssa M. Curry
Copy Editor: Alyssa M. Curry
Cover Artwork By: Gina Startup

ISBN Paperback: 978-1-941711-10-1
ISBN E-Book: 978-1-941711-11-8
ISBN Hardcover: 978-1-941711-09-5
Library of Congress: 2014958445

For information regarding special discounts for bulk purchases of this book for educational, gift purposes, as a charitable donation, or to arrange a speaking event, please visit: www.seraphbooks.com.

www.toddjamesmyers.com
twitter@MyersGma
www.facebook.com/todd.myers.1420

There are countless men and women that take the fall and never get up. We must encourage them to rise with the strength God has given each of us.

–Todd James Myers

Dedication

First and foremost, I want to thank God for healing my heart and giving me another chance at life. He opened my eyes and gave me the strength to understand and endure it all. Only then was I able to let go of everything. When I was broken and stripped down to a minimum, God filled me with light.

Thank you Mom for always believing in me and loving me. You always had faith that I could turn it all around and accomplish anything. You showed me that dedication and hard work would help me achieve my dreams. I could never ask for a better mother.

I want to thank my children. The love you have in your eyes when I look at each of you was my inspiration to become a better man and father. The connection I have with you is priceless and I've never doubted your love. I wouldn't be here without you.

Kelly, thank you for always having time for me and taking me in when I was at my worst.

Troy, when it came to strength and achieving your goals, you were a role model to me.

Dad, thank you for holding on and establishing a stronger relationship with me. It took courage, which taught me that it is never too late.

Denny, thank you for your amazing insight and words of wisdom. You stepped in and lifted up our family when we needed it most. You were that missing piece.

I love you.

Acknowledgements

Although you may not have known the impact you've had on my life, I want to thank you for being there in my darkest hours. When I returned to the light, you allowed me to do so without judgment.

The Diablo Valley Ranch for providing a place that made me feel as close to God as possible.

The counselors: Henry, Cliff, Ms. Ivy, Mike, both Tom's, and James for understanding the truth about addiction and me.

You've had a tremendous impact on my life Auntie Pam, my cousins Scott and Kim, Mike (Turd), my step-mom Bev, and Uncle Kevin.

There were police officers that treated me the same in every room and offered hope when I needed it most.

To everyone I've ever crossed paths with from the dark side that never came to the light.

Anyone I've ever hurt and treated unfairly, please forgive me.

To my eldest child's mother, I am sorry. Thank you for picking up the slack when I fell.

My teacher, pastor, and incredible role model Nancy, you are so good at keeping me balanced. Thank you for being so sweet.

Marala, you are an angel.

There are people that touch your life wherever you go, acknowledge the gift that they've given you and use it to shape your life into something better.

Foreword

During our lifetime, we will face some form of adversity and it may hit us so hard that we take an unexpected fall. Throughout my life, I've seen many encounter unimaginable challenges, but the difference is there are some people who fight to overcome them while others release their faith and completely let go. The choice *is* ours.

Todd James Myers has courageously shared his personal journey in this heart-wrenching narrative that takes us into his ominous world. It warns us about the dangers that are waiting to devour our lives if we allow it. He teaches us how painful experiences can cause us to become a victim of life, render us afraid to fight, and evade the beautiful destiny that God intended for each of us.

The depth of the emotions Todd relived in order to share his story is quite humbling. However, I am certain that his journey will help alter someone's path or save someone's life. *The Fall* will make you examine your own existence and determine how you've handled pain and adversity. It will help you understand why a relationship with God is the most significant one you will ever have. Additionally, it will encourage you to let go of pain and offer forgiveness.

The Fall reveals what can happen to children plagued with physical, mental, and emotional abuse and how they become predisposed to a worldwide problem. People struggle to overcome addiction, but it is avoidable. Todd's journey will help you better understand your own or that of someone you love. Although many will take the fall at some point, it is not meant for anyone to stay down. Todd shares the secret to regaining your faith, happiness, and love for life when you believe all hope is lost. *The Fall* is filled with the power and inspiration to make you get up and live again!

With Love,
Marala Scott

Introduction

There are times I'd find myself watching people in a restaurant, at an event, or someplace random. I usually sit at a table sipping on water with a hint of freshly squeezed lemon, perusing the menu. Often, I opt to try a few items from the selection that seem tempting the way certain aspects of life are. I never know what's going to satisfy my appetite and I'm rather keen on being surprised.

Saturated in my thoughts, I'd rest my gaze upon someone that interest me and ponder away, curious as to what secrets their life held. It doesn't matter where I am; I'll relax in a chair or stand by and reflect while studying the furtive language most people overlook and others try desperately to conceal. Regardless of how beautiful, serious, gentle, cold or dark their eyes are, they reveal something that just can't be hidden; their soul. As I look more intimately, I can't help but to ask myself *if they've ever fallen.*

For some, it's quite palpable for me to sense there is something greater behind the unyielding façade they uncomfortably wear. With others, I can't detect a thing. Like a chameleon, they've hidden their truth for so long, it remains imperceptible until their primary color returns or they miscalculate their next move. Then, there are those who have found peace because they've confronted their past and wisely reconciled the internal and external conflict.

I find the depth of history many people transport from one day to the next utterly inconceivable. It's impossible to know precisely what someone is thinking and what makes them who they are unless we've walked each step of their journey, sinking, stumbling, and falling every time they do. Even then, taking their journey doesn't allow passage inside their head or better yet, soul. You would have to dissect their true intentions, thoughts, beliefs, rational, and everything that makes their mind draw conclusions. The extraordinary thoughts that the subconscious mind creates are what cause actions to be set into motion. Our thoughts shape our life.

It took years of grueling pain, ravaging destruction, self-medicating, and living in life's gutter before realizing I'd been hand-sculpted since I was a child. Even more astonishing, I didn't know what made me Todd James Myers until I'd gone through it all. After gasping for air on the other side, I ascended where I could finally look down from the bridge and see everything more clearly.

With time and edification, I watched the replay of my life and learned who I was and why. Prior to my unsavory experiences, it seemed implausible to know precisely what shapes a person for better or worse. We think we know, but there are always forgotten factors. Genetics, environments, and history help form your personality, shape your thoughts and manufacture fears. If you could see and hear a replica of who you will become, would it persuade you to make the necessary changes? Either way, you are who you are because history doesn't lie and traces of your past often linger. Allow them to be reminders of the individual you do not wish to emerge as later in life and only solicit positive thoughts to ensure it.

As I walked down the street, sat in a café, or interacted with others, I used to wonder what people thought when they observed me. Why? There were times that I didn't know what to think when I examined my own reflection in the mirror. I had moments where I saw a frightening skeleton or flashes of absolutely nothing. Both were significant as they revealed where I was in life.

As for a physical description of myself, I'm six-foot-five, two hundred and twenty-five pounds with dirty blonde hair loosely scattered on my face. I used to wear a mask with a broad smile to hide my pain. I only knew of one way to discard it, which wouldn't happen until I made the decision to face my demons head on. But at the speed I was traveling, I didn't believe I'd survive the collision.

Facing my demons meant acknowledging they were there and determining what led them to me. It was the only way I believed I could rid myself of them. When I was finally prepared to seek the truth, I suspected if I went into the deepest and darkest cavernous area inside of me, I'd find it, along with the resolution. Long ago I had hidden them so I wouldn't have to deal with either.

Once I approached the point that my soul was buried in pain, it became easier to blame others because I wanted to believe that they had earned it. The real problem was that I held them responsible for my actions. My life spun out of control because I felt it was justified. I was given one angry reason after another until they twisted into distorted excuses and finally compounded, rendering me completely toxic.

Though it took me a long time to understand, our personal history doesn't define who we are from one waking day to the next. What defines us is how we defy the errors of our past and whether or not we work diligently to shape our future. We are not the label society gives us; we are only what we believe we are. Since I believed them, I was destined to take *the fall.*

One

1~One~1

In a suburb of the San Francisco Bay Area is where I resided. Like me, it was rich with inconceivable history. It was a place that created memories close to my heart with people that will never be forgotten. Although I failed to notice it for quite some time, the natural landscape was undeniably breathtaking. Every detail and semblance of beauty is etched in my mind like a vivid Norman Rockwell painting. What I hadn't predicted was the drought that manifested inside of me.

I can't really claim I *lived* in Pleasanton because I barely existed. I remained cognizant that each breath of air I inhaled wasn't my own. It was borrowed because I reached a point when life didn't flow through my narrow veins, only pain, laced with destruction.

The Fall

The winter temperatures weren't always friendly and I was beginning to drift from one friend's home to another just to have a place to sleep and shower. When Mom found out, she helped with my hotel rooms here and there but it didn't solve the problem long-term. Eventually, they would kick me out because of the steady flow of clientele I had trampling in and out of my room.

I spent six months at Diablo Valley Ranch, which was my fourth rehab program for addiction. When I was allowed, I'd visit Mom and in less than a month, I started using again. In the program, there are twelve steps to recovery. I didn't complete the twelve steps because I never passed the fourth one. The fourth step is meant to bring up everything you've ever experienced. I was supposed to reveal anything that was burdening me since childhood and turn it over to God. The purpose is to make amends for any harms, fears, and resentments towards others or myself. It's not easy and it can take months to achieve the value of that step. Unfortunately, when I left, I hadn't released what I was carrying inside of me, making it impossible to heal.

My family embraced me when I got out. It was evident they wanted me to succeed so I intentionally did everything for everyone else. It still wasn't for me yet. My family, money, and job weren't making me feel the way I needed to, which was whole again. As soon as life became somewhat challenging for me, it exposed how far removed I was from being rehabilitated and accepting the veracity of my state of mind. I slipped right back into my familiar routine while trying to keep up the façade that I was okay.

Because Mom thought I was doing better after rehab, she made sure that I had my own place, which should have encouraged me to do better. It was a beautiful villa with a pool in a gated community. I had two bedrooms and one bath. The yard was small, but it had a few trees for shade, a shed my mother had built, and a gate for privacy.

Most people that have a shed in their yard use it to store tools. I led my mother to believe I needed it for extra storage but I wanted it for something else. It had a window, concrete floor, old sofa, and a television. Most of the time, I'd sit in there and play Madden with my buddy Hank or I'd go out there to cook meth and escape reality. Even though we both had problems, I could walk away knowing Hank had my back and likewise. My girl, Rosalyn, was like that too, but I didn't want her more involved than she already was. Our romance was centered around the drugs.

Being an addict forced me to experience more than I ever imagined or cared to. You can't use or buy drugs without seeing the truth because you already know you're doing something wrong. Denial was the factor that kept me from fixing the problem.

It was the beginning of fall in 2000 and I'd previously been arrested several times for fraud, drug trafficking, possession, and theft. Upon my release, there was this one cop that was persistent with his attempts to encourage me. Every time I saw him, he warned me that if I didn't get out of the streets, he'd throw me back behind bars for a long time. Jail and prison were two different environments. I tried not to cross the line and end up in prison because I knew I'd become lost in the system. One felony on these charges would be 365 days of jail time. Just one day more, my time would have been served in prison.

The Fall

The last time I was arrested for grand theft, a detective threatened to send me to prison for several years if I didn't become a confidential informant. He told me that I had to give him one big bust or three small ones. I didn't think I had a choice. I snatched my freedom and agreed to help him although I didn't have any intention of doing it the way he wanted or within his parameters.

I didn't know who was worse, the cops, dealers or addicts. The cops wouldn't hesitate to push us into a dangerous situation and if we ended up behind bars or dead, it would only be a reprieve to some of them. They were trying to get us off the streets by fighting a war on drugs. In time, I learned that they couldn't do their job without acquiring information from people on the streets and in the trenches.

Although I had over three hundred thousand dollars touch my trembling hands within a year, those little deals didn't come close to wetting their gluttonous appetites. They didn't want me. The police were mindful of the enormous picture being painted somewhere in their city. They *needed* me along with others, in my unfavorable state, to help them find the artists. I was being exploited to investigate criminal collusion.

The criminals sending drug activity and destroying the city were invisible and it would stay that way until they became sloppy or arrogant. The bigger issue was that the drugs were creating an unwanted landscape for crime. With its constant expansion, the cops were at a loss as to its exact origin of meth labs, and they should have been because there were always more than a few. As for the key players, they weren't well-versed on that either, which caused me to wonder who really had the power. They had the silver badges and alleged jurisdiction, but couldn't put an end to what they weren't able to find. It's easier to locate drugs when you desperately need them.

The key players didn't live in Pleasanton. They were far too clever for that. They simply used smaller towns, cities and rural areas because they were easier playgrounds. Why? Law enforcement was at a minimum. And if they shut down an operation, another one was already being established.

Already in debt to the drugs, I was sick of the police using me too; nevertheless, the poor choices I made depleted my options. Cops believe in the theory that revenge is the best reason to use an informant, and they're right. Unfortunately for them, I didn't operate that way. The more they forced my involvement, the more they believed they were able to have me turn on anyone I didn't like.

Beleaguered by incessant darkness, it became difficult to find a way out of what I was now a part of. Threats by the police offered the same risks as my addiction, and both were greater than being in jail. I'd long accepted the inevitability of death so I continued to dwell where I was most comfortable. Calculating the date and time didn't make sense because death would take me when it was ready.

I wasn't a saint, but the guys they had me connect with were scary. They knew more about drugs than a pharmacist and they had an arsenal of weapons. Besides, the money they handled was out of my league. They were hardened criminals that wouldn't think twice about lodging a bullet in my head.

I was barely twenty-four when I began dealing with significant amounts of money and drugs; that's when the guns came out. One day, I sold five pounds of Mary Jane for eleven thousand dollars. Just a couple hours prior, I had it fronted to me for seven thousand. When you have the right hook ups and you're in touch with people that have the connections, it gets scary. As long as I wasn't buying much I wouldn't reach the real connections of heavy hitters. Heavy hitters equated to prison so I was content on my level.

There were places I went to make deals only to find three hundred pound Mexicans in Mexico and Arizona guarding their supply of Bale Bud that came in two and a half pound bricks. When I placed it on top of a plastic hefty bag it literally peeled apart like hay bales and expanded. If I made a sizeable purchase, I took my own scale so I could measure the drugs accurately. Sometimes their scales were altered.

Drugs will make you do some pretty desperate things but I didn't see it that way at the time. When I needed cash, I made decisions that could have gotten me killed. I'd buy powdered sugar because it looked like pill dope or meth. I'd bag it up, drop it in their lap while they were sitting in their car, collect my money, and disappear. I didn't wait for them to try it either. My activity was so heavy that I didn't expect to see them again. The best people to rip off are addicts or dealers because they can't go to the cops. I took that fifteen dollars I used for the powdered sugar and turned it into fifteen hundred in just three or four days.

Several of the guys I knew or crossed paths with flirted with being a lifer, which meant they only needed one more strike to end up in prison for life. I didn't want to go that deep, which is why I refused to offer much information. The more I'd give, the more they'd push and threaten until I was trapped inside of their world. I'd been beaten by dealers and received death threats trying to retrieve information for the cops; it wasn't worth it.

I didn't expect to be in my own depressing rotation either. The cycle the cops had me running wasn't any different than being an addict; I needed the drugs and they needed me. They let me do whatever I wanted without arresting me so that I could stay in the mix of things and keep my ear to the streets. At one point or another, I either had warrants for my arrest or charges pending, which kept me caught up in the system. Since I wasn't doing anything to change, the cops owned me as long as they wanted. When you enter the game there aren't too many people you can trust, but those you can, you keep. I considered the guys I supplied my friends and I wasn't going to betray any of them to save myself. The guys that supplied me provided the means for me to take care of my meth habit. They hadn't given me any reason to turn on them either. The only thing I could do was utilize whatever creativity I could to conjure up a scheme that would lead the cops in the wrong direction. They'd end up finding something because drugs were everywhere.

After I signed a contract to be an informant, it just so happened that I was arrested the next day. I had to make contact with the detective I was working with so he knew what was going on. Fumbling for an excuse, I'd make up something to keep him from questioning my reliability. If he thought I'd fall through on the contract, he'd arrest me.

I was hiding out at home because I didn't want to run around with those people. I wanted everything to go away because it felt like I'd already gone too deep. Regardless, the cops continued hammering on my door because they wanted me to stay in the game. I told them there were quite a few people that didn't trust me. Before I could go asking questions, I'd need at least a week or more to even connect with the right people. Due to my alleged involvement with the cops, they were hiding from me. I had to acquire drugs through the friends I partied with until people began to trust me again. It was like playing a video game, making it five levels ahead and then being knocked back to level one. Hell, it seemed like everybody was getting knocked back to level one after a while.

The bottom line, I wasn't screwing the cops. If they made a concerted effort, they'd find something. All I needed to do was keep them away from my connections. It appeared to work, but I was running out of ideas and convinced it wouldn't be too long before they caught on.

On New Year's Day in 2001, I woke up to find my body sopping wet and my mind shrouded with fear. I lifted my head and glanced into the dirty kitchen only to find the usual. A sink filled with unwashed dishes, open boxes of cereal, and several empty bottles with a black label were scattered on the Formica countertop. The trash was overflowing and the place reeked. The open white blinds on the sliding glass door leading to the patio allowed the bright daylight to slip in and irritate my eyes. Using my fingers, I combed through my oily, cropped hair and blearily rubbed the sleep from my eyes. Again, I tried to focus as though I was expecting to be someplace else. When I saw the phone I'd ripped out of the wall just hours prior, I realized I wasn't.

I'd been up for nearly five consecutive days with the potent assistance of methamphetamines lingering in my system. Gripping my stomach was all I could do since the pain of withdrawal was seizing what was left of me.

Expecting to catch sight of Rosalyn lying about, I looked around, but instead there was an eerie silence. This time, she was gone and I didn't care. I had other things to worry about like the warrants for my arrest. At the moment, my body hadn't caught up with the dull message my brain was attempting to send. Seeing as it wasn't possible to move, I was forced to lay there a while longer until something registered.

I couldn't remember why I went back home when parties were in full swing, but it didn't matter, I had to pull myself together and get out of there before it was too late. If I didn't, the cops would find me.

The fight I had with Rosalyn the night prior wasn't worth the headache. Now, I was lying on the floor trying to piece it all together but the visions were too blurred. Sharp fragments of threats being hurled between us were all I could recall. I had my demons and Rosalyn had hers but together, the combustion caused our relationship to burst into flames. When I didn't give her the response she required, her ferocity was instantly ignited and her threats came soaring at me like razor-sharp knives.

The Fall

Rosalyn was five-foot-eight and had long, thick curly blonde hair. She was an attractive and educated woman, except she wasn't using it in the capacity she should have. In spite of her own vices, she wasted time trying to save me from myself as if she could somehow love me back to life. She let me stay at her home when I needed it until I had my own. Even with her fury and clouded passion, she looked out for me. Her compassion allowed her to understand why I was out there, but she never acknowledged her own reasons.

Whenever Rosalyn was absorbed in her thoughts or trying to process something, she had an obvious tell. She'd smooth her hair off her face, twist it up into a bun and insert three large bobby pins to hold it in place. My tempted eyes followed her every move when she placed her hands on her swaying hips and sweetly paced the floor. When she spoke to me, her seductive hazel eyes could get her nearly anything she wanted. And her soul, although scarred, was beautiful. Regardless of how hard she tried to help me, it wasn't working and we both knew it. That's why I made an effort to stay away as much as I could.

Forcing myself off the floor, I felt as if I'd been in the cage with a professional kick boxer. The slightest movement and every breath I took brought agony, even when I tried to think. It was a standard routine for me to put a padlock on the front gate and deadbolt my door, but this time, the front door was left ajar. My mind was in a haze, but that still didn't make sense, especially since the police were looking for me. Evidently, Rosalyn must have been in a rush when she left.

Attempting to shake off the sickness and non-functioning mindset, my consciousness hadn't arrived. Still dithering in a state of confusion, I rubbed my eyes and after feeling mild tremors, glanced at my hands. Disgusted by the pungent lingering stench wafting about, I shook my head and tightened my lips, turning them down at the ends. It didn't take long before realizing I contributed to the odor.

Ignoring the open door, I staggered into the bathroom and over to the toilet. To obtain some relief from the nausea, I took my index finger and shoved it down my throat to vomit, and then turned on the shower. Still feeling lethargic and nauseous, I leaned against the counter and looked in the mirror. My eyes were blurry and my vision wasn't clear but when I leaned in for a closer look, I wasn't there. I hoped it was nothing more than a hallucination. I turned on the faucet, cupped my hands together, closed my eyes tightly, and splashed cold water across my face a few times. When I opened them, I jumped back after seeing the reflection of my skull.

"What the hell!"

Trying to compose myself, I rubbed my eyes and took another look. This time, I could see the reflection of the bathroom walls, the shower, and blue towels hanging on the rack, but I still wasn't there. For years I was empty inside until darkness took over. Now, my body was missing.

"Where'd you go?" I mumbled.

I removed the grimy clothes covering my body, dropped them freely to the floor, and stared at them for a moment as a wave of familiar pain swept through me. I saw a vision of my younger self curled up, naked, and crying on the floor. I quickly glanced over my shoulder expecting to feel a powerful blow rendered to the back of my head, but no one was there. Cautiously, I stepped into the shower emitting a sigh of relief.

The water was barely tolerable against my skin but it wouldn't take long before I'd become used to it. I rinsed my hair back off my face and stood stock-still watching the water evaporate into dense steam shrouding the large mirror. While hard streams of water attacked my aching body, I began discharging the poison inside of me again. When I glanced down, I was standing in my own vomit until it slowly spiraled down the drain. Quick flashes of the night before resounded in my clouded and befuddled head like a silent film.

Meth had become the most significant drug threat in Northern California because it was cheap and available in large urban areas as well as in smaller rural communities. The counties south and east of the San Francisco Bay Area were major hubs for its production and distribution.

I was headed to the Reaper's place twenty miles away because I previously told him I needed to make a purchase of his high purity grade meth. He had multiple labs throughout the area and I could tell he had interest in grooming me to be a part of his operation. Every time I stopped by, his security seemed to increase. The last time I was there, he had four six-foot tables stacked with cash like they were printing it, alluding to him being a part of something much bigger. His team was packed with heavy hitters bringing in anything an addict would want and the arsenal of guns he kept in his basement could supply a small army. The Reaper was building his business in the streets out of the clientele living in them, but he had even more in the wealthier parts of town. Those addicts were masquerading as businessmen and housewives that couldn't escape temptation. He didn't care who they were. His focus was on money and nothing else. He never used, drank or so much as smoked a cigarette but the scent of currency was the Reaper's cocaine. I'd proven my loyalty over the past year without bringing trouble to his operation. If I did, he'd kill me.

Anyone close to me knew the police were trying to use me as an informant because I told them. There was no way in hell I'd betray any of them although it hurt that a few didn't accept me. I could tell others felt obligated to help me because they assumed if they didn't, I'd rat them out. I tried to stay two steps ahead of trouble. Instead of having someone communicate the wrong information about me, I set the facts on the table and became transparent. At first, several of my connections dropped back making it clear they didn't want anything to do with me, which was expected. But in time, those like the Reaper understood the value of the knowledge I had access to. Eventually, I was able to jump levels again.

There were dealers funneling thousands of dollars worth of drugs into Pleasanton and surrounding areas. Having someone that knew where the police and DEA were looking kept them relocating their operations or informed when their enemies were about to be eliminated from the game. The Reaper was aware I had more than enough reasons and opportunities to give him up like some of the others had done, but it wasn't my style. The way it worked was if you tried and failed, you'd end up cut off or dead.

The Fall

In time, one of the many disadvantages I had was being a tweaker. I knew where all five of the donation drops were for the Salvation Army in Pleasanton. Tweakers knew when it was drop time. We'd hit it up, trade that stuff for drugs, and go on a binge lasting anywhere from three to fifteen days. When I felt good, I was really out of control. I'd strap a flashlight to my forehead, grab a five-gallon bucket of nuts and bolts and just root through it all night long. One particular time, it was six in the morning before I stopped. It escaped me that I'd been given money the night before to get meth for some of my regulars.

Prolonged use of meth caused me to reach the status of becoming a tweaker. I didn't have control of my emotional or physical state and because of it, I didn't have the attention span to work with the Reaper. He wasn't around when I'd fall into my own world. It was impossible for anyone to have an idea of what was going on in my chaotic head from one moment to the next. Sometimes, I'd take things apart and my mind couldn't process how to put them back together. I'd hide my drugs, forget where and then go insane tearing up the place to find them. Even my behavior had a broad range. Normalcy wasn't part of my existence. I had pockmarks from scratching incessantly and picking at my skin. The hallucinating, uncontrolled repetitive motions, anxiety, and no one's favorite, paranoia, made me look unstable after binging. If something agitated me, I needed to be left alone and Rosalyn knew it. I was headed in the direction of not having any value to the cops because I was unpredictable and it was becoming more difficult for them to reach me.

1-One-1

I had enough control, anger, and emotional abuse inflicted upon me to last a miserable lifetime. I decided that I would no longer accept being burdened with someone's pain because I was already a hoarder of it. I didn't have anywhere to store it, so meth and Jack were my way of attempting to bury it. I hoped it wouldn't re-emerge, but it always did. Each time, the memories were more intense, requiring more substances to repress them.

I made an effort to solicit some sort of comprehension. As though that would restore my memories of the night before, I turned around and allowed the water to flush across my face. Submitting to the hazy recollections creeping back, I released a long moan as I recalled what happened.

Ten minutes later, I was ready to head right back into the devil's playground. I had more to do, but this time I planned on making some significant changes. I had on a pair of jeans and was pulling a white t-shirt over my head as I entered the living room. Once I could see, I froze and quickly threw my hands in the air.

Eight cops had rushed through the front door in their tactical gear, fully armed with guns drawn, simultaneously shouting orders.

"Don't move, Myers!"

"Get your hands behind your head now!"

"Get 'em up! Do you have any weapons on you?"

I only needed one person to tell me, but they were screaming like the defensive line for a football team.

Before I collected a single thought, they were clearing the house. I knew two of them and it wasn't the first time they came to arrest me. But this was different.

The Fall

Det. Jack Branson came through the door behind them. There were times that he crossed boundaries, claiming he was doing his job by any means necessary and I was nothing more than a means. Close to retirement age, he stood six-foot-four, approximately two hundred and sixty-five pounds, with yellow teeth and a faded brown mustache due to sun exposure. His chain-smoking, coffee breath smelled. His expression suggested he'd grown weary of our forced encounters and it should've been obvious that I was too. Branson didn't need to analyze me or ask if I had used because he already knew the physical state I'd be in. In a gravelly tone, he moved closer and tapped my right shoulder to get my attention. My mind was bouncing all over the place.

"How you doin', Todd? You're lookin' a little dark around the eyes."

He noticed me rocking back and fourth but I was trying to shun the painful sensation riding through me.

I shrugged affably and mumbled, "I'm–I'm fine."

My appearance was rough, but since it didn't matter what I put inside me, I didn't care. He looked a little dark around his eyes too. All I wanted to know was *why* they were there. Before I could ask, two of the cops forcefully apprehended me and slammed me back on the floor I struggled to get up from less than thirty minutes prior. A sizable cop yanked my hands behind my back and tightened the cuffs around my wrists, causing me to release a loud grunt.

"Stand him up," Branson ordered.

After observing Branson's bleak expression, I was baffled. Okay, so I hadn't given him the information he wanted. He asked about some guy named Grimaldi, but I doubt it was about that because this seemed more serious.

"Can you at least tell me what this is about? I mean S.W.A.T, Detective? You know I'm not a risk."

"After what we observed last night, I'd disagree."

My expression fell blank and his eyebrows arched together as he studied my face.

"You have no idea why we're here this time?" he asked narrowing his eyes suspiciously.

"No! That's why I'm askin'," I replied. Although the cravings for meth were intensifying, I knew better than to volunteer any information. I let him talk first.

"We executed a couple of warrants on your pals last night."

"My pals? What?" I mumbled, trying to make sense of what he was saying. My stomach boiled with toxic and sour nausea while beads of nervous perspiration covered my twitching brow. Annoyed that I couldn't scratch it, I stood there listening to accusations I seriously didn't know anything about.

"I've tried to work with you. But instead, you've played games–cleverly circumventing the terms of our agreement."

"What? No, I haven't. I–" I began defensively, leaning in towards Branson. Two of the cops quickly raised their guns and moved in closer. "Really guys? Is that necessary? I'm handcuffed!"

"Cut the bullshit! Your game is over and the contract is void from this point. We no longer require your half-assed assistance as an informant," Branson said.

"Now why's that? What'd I do?"

"It's what you haven't been doin'. You're just full of tricks aren't you? Well, I hope you're pleased with

17

your little stunts deflectin' our attention away from your drug-dealin' pals," he said clapping his hands. "You haven't given us shit."

"No! See that's where you're wrong. I've done what you've asked and I've been checkin' around. I just haven't found anything yet."

"What'd you do? Call your buddy Grimaldi and give him a heads up? You sure as hell didn't call me."

"Somethin' came up and I–I lost track of time. You always say you don't give a damn about my personal life so I didn't bother tellin' you."

"Is that so?" he replied, leisurely pacing the living room floor. "Well Grimaldi's timing was pretty damn good. We got a tip on a location right here in Pleasanton and guess what happened?" He threw his hands in the air mockingly and added, "Why am I sayin' guess? Hell, you know." I stared at him like he was crazy because I didn't know. "We get there to raid the place and nothin'. Absolutely nothin'! No drugs. No guns. No money. And no fuckin' Grimaldi! Now I've got my ass on the line with this shit. I think you tipped him off and that's why I didn't hear from you."

"He's working for him, Detective," added one of the cops standing a few feet behind Branson like he wanted to blow my head off.

"What? No! I don't work for him! I wasn't at Grimaldi's place because I don't know him! That's the truth. I swear!"

"Really? His place was surrounded with DEA and FBI. This would've been one hell of a raid!" he announced animatedly. He reached in his pocket and pulled out a pack of cigarettes. While tapping one out, he asked again, "You don't know this guy? Never been to his place?" He slipped the cigarette between his lips, returned the pack to his pocket, pulled out a lighter and lit it.

"No," I said shaking my head.

"Let me guess. You were here playin' Madden," he said, picking up the controller on my coffee table. He shook his head and tossed it back down.

He took a long drag while staring at me with unadulterated distain and then exhaled. What the hell was he talking about? My head wasn't clear but this put me at a complete loss. It sounded like he was trying to set me up.

"Look Detective–"

"You never told us about him and his large-scale production of methamphetamines or his impressive supply of arms. And the money–that's another story. It makes me wonder what else you've been concealing."

"Nothin', because I don't know him and I wasn't at his place. I don't know what he does–and I don't know anything about a supply of arms!"

"Is that so?"

Branson let out a sarcastic chuckle but I didn't get his twisted humor.

"Yeah, it is. You asked me to get Grimaldi's address and I don't have it yet."

"You're worthless to me."

"Like hell I am! I know you found somethin'. And when you page me, I call you within ten minutes just like you told me to. Com'on, you know me."

Trying to appeal to their need for informants on the street was useless. Informants were everywhere and they were probably watching me too.

"We're goin' after these drug dealin' scumbags comin' here to destroy this city. Grimaldi–the cartel–

they're settin' up camp and you won't send us anywhere near them. Now why is that?"

"I-don't-know-that-guy!"

I couldn't say it any other way. And I could tell by the look on his face that he didn't believe me. None of them did.

"You really think you can outsmart us Trick Bag? You can't. You don't deserve my help and that's what I've given your sorry ass. I only did it because of Carp. He *claimed* you had it rough. But if you think you've had it rough, try thinkin' about someone other than yourself for a change, like Carp's sister. It's time you hit the pavement so you can see how hard it is. If it's behind bars, maybe *then* you'll get up. You did this to yourself. The only way to keep your sorry ass out of prison was to use you as an informant and you couldn't even do that right. You've violated our deal and crossed the fuckin' line I warned you about. Last night we ran simultaneous raids not only here but two counties over where Grimaldi lives. The place was said to be a loaded fortress."

"I don't know anything about a fortress and I can't tell you what I don't know. If you have Grimaldi's address why are you even here? You don't need me."

"My sentiments exactly. For months, you've sent us all over the Bay Area on scavenger hunts to avoid hitting Grimaldi as well as others. Your scheme wasted taxpayer money and our time along with it. You should've worked with us. But now–we're done. Because you think you're a fucking smartass, our deal's over. Todd James Myers, you're under arrest," Branson stated. He bit down on his bottom lip staring at me coldly before adding, "I can't help you. Not anymore." He turned to an officer, dismissively threw his hand in the air and said, "Take him."

This didn't make sense. I must have been set up.

Branson indicated that he was working with other state and federal law enforcement agencies, which meant this was big. If it was big, it didn't have anything to do with me. I stayed away from it to avoid this! He thought he could use me to dig deep enough to benefit him on a larger scheme of things but that wasn't my arena and he could tell by my lifestyle. They didn't care about anything other than the results. I was being charged with multiple felonies and I didn't know my fate. They lowered my head and put me in the car. I looked out the window of the squad car as it pulled off and wondered who was playing games.

The Fall

Two
My Dark Reality

It wasn't long before I was back in a cold familiar place, behind bars with three hots and a cot. For most of us, once we were on the inside, we submitted to it being a necessary break. We had time to detoxify and think. Being in jail didn't necessarily mean we were going to change for the better. It presented time to dissect the foundation that twisted, shaped, and fueled our negative emotions. Doing so had the ability to lead us to *why* we persisted to self-destruct.

I glanced around at my dark reality. There was nothing to it but a cot, sink, toilet, ten feet of space, and a Bible for comprehension and peace. The dim light above the sink never went off ensuring the darkness wasn't in the hole itself but inside of my mind.

The Fall

Supposedly, I was a confidential informant so I should have been in protective custody; however, it was New Year's Day and cold outside. From the middle of November until around March, the jails and rehab programs were crammed packed and there wasn't any room. By the second week in November, people started to self-medicate more than they already had. It was the only way they knew how to release the pain the season appeared to bring. There were men and women that found it impossible to handle their situation, which made the holidays difficult. Some weren't able to provide for their family, lost a loved one, or were addicts. Regardless of the reason, loneliness and history had a way of resurfacing more rapidly.

To ensure my safety until a space opened up, the guards put me in the hole, also known as D-block. Being in the hole wasn't going to help because the longer I was there, the worse my emotional state became. If I were to break, my demons would finish what they started as if I belonged to them.

By eight o'clock that morning, they slid a tray into my cell with a bowl of cereal and a piece of bread. We called it brick bread because it sat three inches high. I thought it tasted better than any bread I'd ever had and it was literally a slice of heaven. Being behind bars forced me to find something that I could look forward to, just for the sake of my sanity, and that bread was it.

I spent the first day curled up on the bed; exhausted, dehydrated, hungry and lost. Inevitably every fiber of my being was craving meth. I felt like I was alone, no different than being abandoned on a deserted island. Overwhelmed by everything that happened, I thought it would help if I could manage to force some tears out. It was similar to having severe nausea but unable to throw up. I was in more pain from the Jack Daniels than meth. Every bit of physical, emotional and spiritual pain had risen to the surface and I was desperate to relieve some of it because it wanted to get out of me, so I began wincing. I'd shut my eyes and then squeeze them tightly waiting for the tears to fall. At that time, I was so emotionally detached because of the run I'd been on that it was difficult to connect to those tears.

I didn't have anyone to bail me out because I did an excellent job of removing the trust from my relationship with Mom. She was exhausted from the lies, along with my unsavory behavior, which had finally proven to be too much for her. I pushed her patience and tested her love to the limits of her own sanity. Even at that time, I understood her tough love approach.

I was hurting my sister, Kelly, and brother, Troy, more than I realized. I couldn't blame them; their little brother was an addict. The irony of the situation was that I found it impossible to determine how my father viewed me now. The bulk of my pain originated from him and he undoubtedly had a specific origin for his own. As much as I hated it, I'd proven to be more like him than I thought; he couldn't handle his pain either. When I looked into the windows to his soul, I could see that he was completely twisted inside and constantly reaching for a bottle of Jack. All I had to do was let it go, but I didn't. As a result, my life imploded.

My dark reality suggested that I spent the majority of my life waiting for someone to save me. I needed someone to acknowledge what caused me to feel defeated and devoured by life and then tell me that it wasn't my fault. Internally, I was begging for the truth to be unveiled and someone to take responsibility for their role in my demise. If they judged their actions instead of mine, then maybe– maybe I'd be able to do the same.

I'd been living in my own prison although I wasn't exactly a victim anymore. I made the choice to cross that boundary and fall out of my life knowing the pits of hell were waiting. I was free falling from the top of Mount Thor. The experiences and lessons of my childhood are what created that alternative. Only people that are broken, weak, destroyed, suffering, sick, desperate or lonely would take that option. They would be depleted of the energy or willingness to fight. And when I saw the bridge, I chose it, even with all of its glowing embers and inviting flames.

I took a deep breath knowing depression wouldn't be unemployed anytime soon. I didn't realize it until much later but it was something I'd been struggling with since I was eight years old. It single-handedly captured my entire consciousness as though it were a simplistic task revered for its masterful invasion.

Finally, my emotional release began. I woke up with tears streaming down my face. I felt flat, like nothing was left except an aching body stricken with the flu. When I turned over, my eyes fixated on the small window cut into the cell door. I got up and stumbled over to it placing my left eye against it, hoping to see some sign of life. I needed to know I wasn't alone. The affects of being in my cell, or the hole, allowed my thoughts to run rampant. I felt disconnected, especially from my family on the streets. It didn't take long before I wanted them to remove me from isolation so I could be a part of something or whatever was going on in the rest of the population.

By the time they allowed me to make a call, I was desperate to talk with someone because it was the only way to pull myself out of the state I was in. A simple exchange of words would make a notable difference. Not being connected to anyone or anything was difficult to handle but being left with my own thoughts was an invite to suicide. The Shawshank Redemption came to mind. "Fear can hold you *prisoner.* Hope can set you free."

Everything had a routine and part of it allowed me to have thirty minutes of call time each day. Rosalyn wasn't taking my calls and I was certain if I didn't talk with Mom, I was going to lose what was left of me. I picked up the phone and dialed Mom. I didn't know if she'd take my call either since I was locked up again. Once, I cooked meth at her house while she was gone. I'd stolen a shotgun from underneath her bed and traded it for an ounce but she still took my calls. Although Mom was sympathetic to me at times, she was being dragged through my pain and suffering in a different way. After I dialed, my heart raced faster every time it rang, but no one answered. I slammed the phone down and yelled, "Fuck!"

"Myers, calm down!" the guard threatened, tightly gripping his baton. "This is the only phone in this area."

Without another word, the guard returned me to the hole. Two stale looking bologna sandwiches and an apple were placed in the cell. I sat on the cot and forced it down. It didn't take long before I started crashing. My body responded like it was tired of being abused and made the sole decision to quit on me. My eyes went in and out of focus staring at the black Bible on the end of my bed until the weight of my eyelids gave in and sleep devoured me.

I woke up in a cold sweat, feeling sick with a hot, tingly sensation creeping up my legs. I didn't know how long I'd slept but it felt like a week. My mental state made it impossible to remember. My leg brushed against something. I glanced towards the bottom of the bed and noticed the open Bible as if I had begun reading it. Feeling nauseous, I rolled off the cot and stumbled over to the toilet, tightly holding my abdomen. I was so weak that those few short steps quickly stole the last of my energy. After vomiting several times, I rinsed the bitter taste from my mouth and curled back up in bed. I couldn't recall if the court-appointed attorney had already come to discuss my case, if so, it must not have been good because I was still locked up.

I shut my eyes and began rocking to try and ease the pain and nausea. My tongue was swollen, teeth were aching, and the sores in mouth were irritating but I had to suffer through it. I didn't have Anbesol to dull the sensation so the only thing that could possibly alleviate it was sleep. Incoherently, I slipped out of consciousness into my nightmares.

I may have been sleeping for hours or days but again, I still didn't have any concept of time. I'd been deprived of sleep so my body took over and forced its own recovery. I could detect a notable change in the environment as though I was no longer in confinement, and then something eerie happened. I was awake and sitting up, like I was working my way out of my body, which was still lying on the cot. I glanced down, unfazed that it was there. Once I understood what was taking place, I became fearful that if I pulled myself too far out of my body I might not make it back. Although it was a paranormal feeling, I conceded because I thought it was better given that I felt at peace about everything. The pain was gone and the cravings didn't exist. That must have meant the hurt I caused others had ended. It was over.

Everything edged towards a serene darkness and then I saw a vision of Jesus sitting at the end of my bed in an off white robe with a brown belt around it. His hair was long and everything about Him was peaceful. Enveloped by the glory of His presence, it made me want to be better because He was there for me. I felt *everything* was going away. Spiritually, my doors had been closed for so long, they too were disappearing. Then, Jesus was gone. Everything was black again.

"Myers! Get up!"

"Huh?" I replied sluggishly opening my eyes.

"Walk," the guard demanded, poking me in the leg with his baton.

I stood up and shrugged. "Really? Where?"

"Walk!" he ordered, forcefully shoving the baton into my aching back. I walked from one end of the tiny cell to the other.

Leaving what items I had on the bed, he yanked the sheet off and then pulled the mattress from its frame, tossing it into the corner. He stirred up my personal belongings as if he were releasing his own hidden aggressions.

He grimaced and yelled, "Now clean this shit up!"

An hour later, a guard slid a tray inside my cell. By the time I finished eating, the same guard came back, removed the tray, and then took me to shower. When I was returned to my cell, I sat idle, trembling for a while. My thoughts had become more defined, as if a light was turned on for me. I could sense the temperate pulsation of my heart again.

I was saddened by what I'd done with my life and to my family. I dropped my head and looked fixedly at the concrete floor. In jail, I didn't have control over anything and that scenario wasn't any different than being on the outside. I never knew what would happen to me out there either.

Time was playing a game with me and I was losing. I had a week to ten days before I'd find out my prison sentence. What the hell was I thinking? It could have been years before I was back with my family. My eyes welled with tears.

"Myers!" I lifted my head to find a pretty sizable guard opening my cell door. "Time to make your call."

I nodded and stood up placing my hands behind my back so he could cuff me. He pointed down the hall to the left, followed me to the phone, and then removed the cuffs. I didn't have time to waste making random calls. Reaching out to Mom again made the most sense, but I was out of luck if she didn't accept the collect call. My hand was trembling when I picked up the phone. I'd been trying to reach someone since I'd been there, but I'd worn everyone out to the point no one took my call. I didn't expect this time to be any different but I had to try.

My Dark Reality

Surprisingly, Mom accepted the call but at first, she didn't say anything, which allowed me to pick up on her unyielding disappointment. I heard a long inhale followed by a deep gradual exhale as if she were preparing for the mendacity. She just listened and contained her thoughts while I tried to explain everything coherently. The more I spoke, it became easier to detect the words resting in her throat, but she didn't say much because she'd said it all before. I begged her to forgive me and told her how incredibly sorry I was.

There are misconceptions when it comes to addiction. For starters, being in pain and destroying my life didn't mean I didn't care, love, or feel anymore. It meant that *I* was in pain. The more I deliberated over the consequences I was facing, the more depressing my situation became.

Concluding a brief conversation with Mom, she asked me not to call so much. Her words were stabbing because I could feel the anguish I caused her and it had been several years in the making. Locked up and waiting to be sentenced provided evidence I was too much for anyone to handle. Although they loved me, they had to move on. It must have been a reprieve for Mom to know I wasn't using. I was getting rest, clean, and more importantly, alive.

As the guard cuffed and escorted me back to the hole, I felt like my heart was caving in. When he took the cuffs off and locked me in, I plopped down on the thin cot and picked up the Bible. The corner of the page was folded down like it had already been marked. Psalms 31 captured my attention. I took a deep breath and began reading.

Quite desperately, I'd been searching for comprehension and peace. I thought I'd find it in the

The Fall

Bible because it definitely wasn't inside of me. I was empty and without wisdom. The words gave me *hope* because I understood the concept of embracing them. Mom taught me how to do that as a child and I learned how to feel them manifest in my soul. I was facing several years in prison and I'd lose my mind if I didn't strengthen my soul. I hoped God knew where my heart was. I hadn't felt it in quite some time. I couldn't allocate blame because every choice that led me there, I made. I knew who I was and being behind bars at that moment was where I belonged. While I didn't believe it was Branson's intent, jail was a blessing and it wasn't in disguise. It was meant for me to go through withdrawals, sober up and come to terms with the direction of my life or what was left of it.

Hours blended into a few more days and time kept rolling along without me. Rather than sitting in the hole thinking about my mistakes, if it were possible, I wanted to determine how to fix them and where to begin. I needed to calm my thoughts and it was natural for me to find solace in reading the Bible. Every time I woke up, I went right back to it and read one passage after another. If I didn't understand something, I'd go back, read it again, and think about it until I did. I didn't know it at the time, but it was almost as if I was reprogramming myself. In between reading, I'd pray, cry hysterically, and then continue. I don't know how long I sat on the cot with the Bible in my hand, but there came a point when I knew it was time.

I stood up, lifted my hands in the air, and called out for God to hear me. I belted out the hardest plea I had because I wanted to get out everything I needed to say. Some of the words were from long ago, but they needed to be expunged. I cried harder than I thought possible. Suddenly, I felt something resembling the onset of a storm activated by thunder crashing inside of me.

A lucid vision of being in a boundless, grassy field observing the branches of a massive oak captured my attention. Surrounded by complete serenity, it dawned on me that I was looking at my family tree. The extended branches were uniquely twisted and had the names of each family member carved into them. There were other branches with the names of anyone that was close to me. The message became clear and left me more humbled and broken than I'd ever been. My body fell limp. I took a fall to my knees, tightly clasped my hands together, and bowed my head, sobbing heavily. That conversation was set in motion a long time ago and it was solely between God and I.

The Fall

Three
Suspended in Thought

The teacher's voice loomed from a distance making it impossible to understand what he was talking about. I was leaning back as far as I could in my chair with my eyes closed, inaudibly mouthing the words to, *"If I Can Dream"*. As soon as the bell for recess rang, I bolted from my seat to be the first one out of the classroom. I sprinted down the meticulously polished hallway floor wearing my blue and gold Pumas and a blue, stonewashed, crewneck Fonzie t-shirt. When I was within reach of the door, I rotated my body sideways, slid into it and forced it open. The sunshine quickly spread across my face like a picket fence being whitewashed, but I didn't have time to enjoy it. Seven or eight of the girls in my third grade class were right behind me. They made me feel important, loved, and handsome, which was the opposite of how I felt at home. It filled me with confidence so naturally I was hooked. At night, I'd fall asleep thinking about how much these girls loved chasing me and it gave me something to look forward to.

In a customary manner, they made a valiant effort to capture me, but it would only ruin the fun if I made it easy. I'd let them tackle me in the lush grass right before they grew tired, disinterested, or gave up. The green leaf volatiles emitted the strong scent of freshly cut grass. Holding down my moist palms, one by one, the girls would kiss my flushed cheeks. I'd squirm around, shaking my head back and forth pretending I didn't like it. Adding another element of fun was the last girl, Mary Bailey. The smell of sour milk permeated her skin while Mary's reputation for picking boogers preceded her. After she'd plant a kiss on my cheek, it seemed as though my strength managed to emerge and I transformed into the Hulk, playfully tossing the girls aside before darting away giggling. Other than the boogers, Mary was pretty nice. She sat next to me in class so we often joked and giggled about stupid things. There were occasions when she didn't have lunch money so I'd bring my change and give her a nickel each time she let me look down her blouse. I would have given it to her even if she didn't.

Everyone has some kind of little personality traits that are good, bad or just weird. I was at a stage where I was learning more about myself, as well as others, and it was fascinating. I wanted to be happy because it felt right. I didn't like conflict and I couldn't handle stress. Therefore, I didn't like watching it occur, causing it, or being a target. At that age, I realized I despised bullies. Bullying is a disgusting display of weak individuals picking on weaker or other defenseless people. It seemed that the unhealthy environment they existed in caused them to mimic hateful behaviors and take it out on others. It gave the impression that it offered them a release of pain while reloading some of their own power from it. I didn't think kids should know anything about pain, but I knew plenty. It wasn't because I chose to learn; I was involuntarily enrolled in the course.

Big Barry was this obnoxious kid that wouldn't stop picking on another classmate. Barry was relentless in calling that kid cruel and demoralizing names while taunting him with malicious pranks every opportunity he could pilfer. The kid was defenseless to Barry and clearly tried to avoid the magnitude of hatred being distributed. He'd fold his arms across his chest and get ready for whatever was going to happen. However, it was apparent that he didn't like it, and neither did I. His body language spoke volumes when he'd hunch over and turn away as if he were praying for Barry to pass him. I watched Barry torment that same boy since the beginning of the school year.

One morning, Barry came to school wearing heavily creased blue jeans, a red and white stripped shirt, and had a fresh buzz cut. He walked around the class pushing books off the desks and flicking kids in the head as he made his way over to that same kid. I quietly sat at my desk observing him. He looked like he was on a mission to pick a fight or humiliate him.

That kid *never* bothered anyone. He was in his own little zone, placidly drawing at his desk before Barry showed up. Barry walked up alongside of him, snatched his pencil, and started running that kid

The Fall

through an emotional shredder. Barry had a lot to get off his chest. The kid tried to get up and move away, but Barry shoved him back down in his seat and kept getting in his face. Some of the kids laughed, most were uncomfortably quiet, but the teacher didn't stop it. She ignored the situation and stepped out of the classroom to talk with another teacher. Big Barry bullied that kid because he was allowed to. For some reason, I believed that if no one put an end to it, the poor kid would hate coming to school and lose faith in people. I could see it in his face. Perhaps, that's how I felt about my life.

All of a sudden, I had an intense recollection of being curled up on the floor while my father balled up his fist and struck me repeatedly. Watching Barry's performance caused me to have an overpowering reaction. My eyes welled up with tears. I wasn't surprised to find myself struck with an overwhelming sense of responsibility to do something. A surge of anger reached a temperature so hot that it boiled out of me.

The more Barry used his words to slash that kid apart, the more I wanted to use my fist to shut him up. I leapt out of my seat like it was on fire, sprung across another desk, and beat him so badly I was suspended for fighting, but I didn't care. I felt *so* good about it because Barry didn't bother him again and he was suspended along with me. I didn't want to be a bully; I just wanted to protect someone the way I wished someone had done for me. I wanted that kid to feel safe.

There were so many negative situations taking place that an escape hatch was necessary every now and then. Climbing a towering ladder out of my life allowed fresh air to pierce through the toxic

38

environment. Being surrounded by nature was an escape and Pleasanton was so beautiful that it offered plenty.

Jumping on my Redline bike and riding it throughout town or playing ball with my friends allowed me to refrain from thinking about much else. I was busy taking advantage of breathing the non-toxic air as if I could take in enough to last me throughout the night. It shouldn't have been any different than the air at home, but it was. It made me appreciate the freedom I had.

School never held my attention for long and I couldn't wait for it to let out. I'd take my time going home so I could hang out with my cousin Scott along with a group of our friends. It was a regular thing for us to stop at the local 7-Eleven and pick up a few snacks. I'd buy a Marathon Bar, Big Hunk or Charleston Chew and washed it down with a Slurpee. We'd talk about school, sports, girls and sometimes situations at home. Despite anyone's personal plight, we made it a point to have fun when we were together. We didn't waste time sitting around complaining about things we couldn't control. Playing football, basketball, baseball, hockey or anything that kept us engaged and laughing is all we ever did. We were far more mischievous than our parents knew but then again, we were kids.

Sometimes people don't know what their value is to others. My time with the guys meant more to me than they would have thought because that's when I was able to block out everything that sparked misery. We'd fantasize about what we were going to be when we grew up and the type of life we'd have. Scott wanted to be an athlete or involved in sports and I had the desire to be a gangster like Scarface. The impact Scarface had made me want to gravitate towards that life. I got chills watching it because it gave me strength and relatability. Gradually, it became a part of my transformation and I loved it. I was unmindful that those incredible times would wane.

When my adventures around town came to a close, regardless of where I was, there were several routes I could take to go home. However, only one held significance to me. I preferred it because it was the longer route that took me over a bridge and across a restless stream approximately thirty feet below. Oak trees, tall grass, daisies, and rocks beautifully landscaped it. I knew every detail of it, calculated its peaceful rhythm, and wanted to believe it knew the truth about me.

Countless hours were spent along the embankment peacefully observing tadpoles darting about in the stream while dragonflies fluttered in the warm air above. The water was deep enough to lie down in and become fully emerged. I found everything about it entrancing, which is why I took my time crossing it. In fact, I used to scale along the outside of the bridge, lightly holding the rail, while taking one step at a time in between each post until I reached the middle. That's where I'd stop, *suspended in thought*. Nothing else mattered.

By the time I arrived home, it was typical for me to have a few hours to myself. Often, Kelly was with her friends and Troy was with his. I'd grab a bowl of cereal, pop tarts or some kind of snack, and ultimately zone out in front of the television watching *Popeye* or the *Bugs Bunny and Road Runner Show*. When my parents came home they'd ask how school was going. I'd tell them everything was good but of course it was fabricated in an effort to buy time to breathe. The truth was that I struggled with focusing on my work, cheated on tests, and frequently got into trouble. My mind was continuously occupied with having to navigate through my home life, which I thought took precedence over everything else. In my world, homework wasn't anywhere on the list.

People see failure without caring to identify the cause and they think kids are stupid. I wasn't stupid, just distracted mentally, emotionally, and physically. Every once in a while, I had a teacher that understood how to connect with me in a way that encouraged me. And precisely what they offered was what I needed. There were a few teachers that didn't toss me into a negative category, lick the label, and quickly apply it. Instead, they determined what areas were most problematic for me, discovered a way to circumvent them, and worked to help me attain a greater level of success. Teachers that were unconstructive or communicated negatively couldn't get through to me because it wasn't any different than what I had at home.

My time ran out whenever Dad learned that I failed a few tests and was having trouble with some of my classes. He'd receive a call from my teacher and then whatever lies I told made facing reality worse. Lying was my only option to prolong an inevitable beating. I learned how to lie as an attempt to protect myself from other things that caused my father's fury. Either way, I still met the consequences. I would not have had a reason to lie if I wasn't living in fear. With enough practice, it became a habit. The key to understanding why someone is lying is to ask *what* caused him or her to avoid the truth. There were too many distractions that made it virtually impossible to concentrate on what should have been important, but again, no one could see inside of my mind. The trepidation that kept me dodging reality seemed invisible to everyone but me. My thoughts were laden with haunting flashbacks and the only other person that could possibly see them was my father. He knew he was hurting me and whoever hurt him was aware of the same.

There are defining moments that teach us to hate or love and others that fill us with anger or peace. I recall the story about my father having a pet goat when he was a child. The goat would stand on its hind legs and take food from his hands. It often slept with him. After school one day, he went home shocked and sickened to find his goat's head chopped off and draining in a bucket. The rest of the goat was boiling in the silver pot on the stove. I wonder what that moment in history taught my father or filled him with because it did something. When Dad shared that story with me, it provided an emotional glimpse into his childhood.

Silence at home should have been comforting, but there was a day when it was considerably daunting. I heard the vibration of nothing until a door slammed shut, rattling my nerves. I waited for him to appear in the doorway. Only moments later, I realized it was a draft from an open window across the hall. Knowing it would happen soon, I sat on the edge of the bed and cupped my hands between my knees. Every little sound caused me to jump in a panic or quickly turn away from the window in the direction of the door. Toiling with the bottom of my white t-shirt was a failed distraction. My legs began to tremble when his wrath was nearly upon me and my spirit had already claimed a cataclysmic defeat. Being terrified of my father caused a heightened response to his presence and I'm sure I wasn't the only person to experience it. The warning that signaled his arrival trickled up my nose like a poisonous gas causing fear to casually seep out of my pores, adding to the fulminating environment. The steady drip of my perspiration was evident that I anticipated it would be worse this time. Kindred to an approaching tsunami, I couldn't do anything to prevent it. I'd wait in my brother's room because I could see if Dad was coming down the street. I don't know why I'd torture myself by staring out the window and submissively wait, but I did. On occasion, Dad arrived home earlier than Mom. When I saw his white utility truck parked in the driveway, my stomach grew sick. Tremors multiplied and shot through me. My aching head was ready to detonate as fear wrapped around me like the tentacles of an octopus squeezing tightly.

Once I heard the side door slam shut, my mouth fell agape, but the air narrowly escaped me. My father's heavy footsteps grew louder as they proceeded in my direction. Then, an inescapable need to vomit hit me. I couldn't run or even move, but soon–I would.

As I sat in silence waiting to see what kind of mood he was in, the day I went into Troy's room and found blood all over his dresser came to mind. Just the thought caused my legs to bounce up and down to the beat of fear. It was a few years prior, but even then, I was terrified of what my father was capable of becoming. I believed that sooner or later it would covet me. Troy was the first to experience it, but by the time I was five, he was persistent in transferring it to me.

A few minutes later, he stood in the doorway of Troy's room wearing a pair of jeans and a flannel shirt. He stared at me while his rage began to work its way out of him.

Clenching his teeth together, I watched the muscles in his jaw pulsate before he stated with a discomforting calmness, "I received a call from your teacher today." I just stared at him wide-eyed expecting the inevitable. "You know what she told me? You're a little liar!"

Responding wasn't an option because he took four aggressive steps towards me, balled up his fist, and threw a solid punch to my head knocking me to the ground. He unbuckled his belt and yanked it off in a swift motion. To indicate he was just beginning, he folded it in half and snapped it. Shouting familiar obscenities, he whipped my frail body, landing the belt anywhere it could strike. Screaming out in pain, I curled into a fetal position pissing all over myself. Trying to flee would have only made things worse. Much worse. By the time he was done, I was beaten, bloody, and soaked in my own urine.

He looked down at me displaying nothing less than sheer gratification and said heatedly, "You stupid fuck," as if I made him beat me.

Mom must have heard Dad's voice attempting to drown out my screeching cries. As soon as the door shut, she raced into the room and found him savagely towering over me gripping his black belt.

Quickly dropping to the floor and scooping me into her arms she yelled viciously, "What have you done? Get out of here you sick son-of-a-bitch! Get away from my son!" When he left, Mom held me for the longest time, crying as hard as I was.

That wasn't the end of it. Time went on as cruel as ever. It brought out the worst and more frequently. The end was nowhere in sight and I'd fallen into a vicious rotation that I couldn't decode.

It was fall of 1976 and by the third grade I was already screwed up. Whenever something felt abnormal or stressful, I'd go into the kitchen, open the cabinet, and pull out the bowls. Then, I'd stack them over and over. Sometimes, I'd walk around rotating my wrists in a quick repetitive motion. It may have appeared as though I were pretending to be in an old western movie, drawing guns from a holster. In actuality, I was casting the pain out of me, the same way a cutter needs to release theirs.

My father administered his anger with absolute disdain. His eyes would narrow quite chillingly as he'd observe me, making it apparent he had a difficult time biting his tongue.

"What are you doing? Knock it off you fuckin' meathead!"

But I couldn't. It was random and didn't have any particular rhythm, it just happened. I'd drop my head in embarrassment and try to stay away from him as much as possible. Emotionally, I was incapable of managing what was going on with me because I didn't have control or the comprehension to understand it all. At times, I appeared happy but internally, I was awaiting darkness to take over so my father could strike. When I felt it infiltrate the environment, regardless of how bad it would be, I just wanted to get it over with. I hated living in a state of having to guess when that time would arrive.

Children shouldn't live under stressful conditions because it is avoidable. But in our home, we avoided the problem and tried to co-exist instead of alleviating it.

By the time I was eight years old, I experienced anxiety as if I were an adult that had been traumatized in some horrifying way. Unable to process everything that transpired became mental and emotional struggles that were overwhelming. Trying to contain or hide it wasn't wise, but I didn't know what else to do. During the most random occasions I'd go into the pantry to grab a box of cereal or do something routine and without warning, everything would go black. My vision would shut off and randomly return.

Worried about the potential for underlying issues, Mom took me to be examined by a doctor. They asked a lot of questions, ran preliminary tests, shaved little patches in my hair, and then hooked wires up to it. Tests revealed the cause was basically, insurmountable stress. I was traumatized by what was happening at home. After additional testing, Mom was told my IQ was 140 or 141. The doctor thought I was passing out due to stress and he probably assumed I was studying too hard. On the contrary, I couldn't study because of the stress.

I returned home and nothing changed. Typically when there is dysfunction in a home, to the degree there was in ours, it doesn't get better. The tension, beatings, and general unhealthy communication evolved until it became intolerable and feasted on me without disruption. I no longer anticipated the approaching stress because by that time, it was always present.

Without warning, my involuntary behaviors would resurface making me look unstable because *I was*. Although I tried, I couldn't hide it. None of my friends said anything about it anyway. When my combination of pain hit an unbearable level, I'd go into the kitchen, yank open a drawer, and grab the sharpest knife I could find. Feverishly gripping the brown handle, I'd push the knife against my abdomen thinking that was the only way to avoid further beatings from my father. I wanted to die but I was too afraid to kill myself. Since I couldn't escape what was happening, thoughts of death consumed me.

One afternoon, I went into my parent's bedroom and saw the gun my father usually kept in his nightstand resting on top of it. He bought me a BB gun that I used down by the stream or when riding my bike. I'd aim at trees and little objects for practice. I didn't consider holding a .38 Special to be any different. I picked it up and pensively stared down its barrel while my mind worked to persuade me to pull the trigger. I could tell the gun was loaded. Before my finger inched towards it, I placed it back down, left the room and gently closed the door.

I felt sickened by my thoughts, which filled me with sadness to understand the concept of my life having lost meaning before it had truly begun. I maintained hope that one day I'd release my fear of death, thrust the knife, pull the trigger, or do whatever I had to.

The pain I carried stemmed from a combination of what happened to everyone in my family, not just me. Every time I witnessed Mom being allocated her portion of my father's verbal storm, it felt like he placed a plastic bag over my head and taped it around my neck to suffocate me while I helplessly watched. I saw her facial expression change as if she were in disbelief that the man she loved had that side to him. If she were afraid, she didn't back down, but I didn't have that strength. Mom was stronger than me because she kept standing. The only time I saw her fall was to pick me up or pray.

There were times that I missed my sister because she'd take me to hang out with her and her boyfriend, Mike, without making me feel like an emotional burden. I went to some phenomenal concerts with them, which caused my passion for music to absolutely explode.

My father didn't seem as angry when Kelly was around. Although they had a better relationship I always thought it was because she was smart enough not to make waves. There were times I wished she were home, but it was better that she was gone, doing what she loved, and away from the madness. I knew that my sister loved me, but she couldn't help me during that time. I didn't talk anymore than necessary or trust the environment. I wore my smile and took it.

Troy and I had more of Mom's features than Dad's. My brother was tall, handsome and intelligent but I only wished I knew him better. Despite our efforts, time wasn't in favor of Troy and I building a stronger relationship. Six years my senior, the majority of my brother's time was spent hanging with his friends or Dad. Things weren't always that way, but as the seasons changed so did their relationship. Time allowed them to adjust to one another, but I was never a part of that equation.

It's been said, the eyes are the windows to the soul. I didn't think anyone, except Mom, knew the color of mine. If they were to look, they'd see the death I was experiencing had turned them from blue to black.

Everything remained the same while my parents continued working to establish their company. They provided overhead and underground power lines that were high voltage. The threat of danger was always imminent and their marriage gave the impression of being unhealthy too. Whether or not they realized it, they'd grown accustomed to their own plight. During the weekdays, Dad was at his worst but when the weekends arrived, they had their share of fun and he was much easier to be around.

The casino was one of the places he seemed to enjoy most. My parents built a cabin in South Lake Tahoe and frequented Harrah's & Harveys. When they left my cousin Scott and me in daycare, we had a great time. They gave us enough quarters to last throughout the night and we spent some of our time watching movies.

With time came acceptance and I took it all in. Watching them taught me how to operate and exist within the confines of impeccable dysfunction. Our house wasn't the only one synonymous with problems. Most people hide theirs and smile politely as they leave their home offering the impression that everything's normal. Several of my friends were dealing with some of the same topical issues we had but the severity remained unknown to me just as mine had to them.

I thought that my parents were more likely to believe or hope I'd grow up and all of the bad memories would wither and die. They didn't consider, hate doesn't go away when the seeds are planted inside of you. The roots would need to be extracted by a professional. Then again, the depth of the roots would determine if that were even possible. Given just a little attention, they could easily be nurtured back to health.

One unspoken facet of my personality was that my parents taught me how to hide everything I felt, just like they did. Mom was good at sharing a radiant smile and Dad was the best at disguising his pain because he hid it in a bottle of Jack Daniels. When they interacted with others, it wasn't as noticeable.

Problems constantly evolved and since they couldn't fix them, they ignored them and continued on with their lives. As beautiful as my mom was, it became obvious she wasn't content. Every time she left the house, I thought she was searching for some piece of happiness because it wasn't inside of her. Consequently, I developed other repetitive behaviors that I couldn't control. Neither of my parents knew what to do with me.

The one thing that I needed the most in life I learned when I turned thirteen. That particular lesson, I'd subconsciously hold onto for the rest of my life whether or not I wanted to. My mother made sure that I understood the concept of *turning your life over to God*. While Mom was quietly searching for peace she got involved with a prayer group from her church and even sang beautifully in the choir. Innately, my mother had a good heart; only I thought pain had been poured into it, like mine. Ultimately, it was her resolute faith that caused me to plant my own mustard seeds at a young age. I didn't know if I'd ever see them come to fruition, however I planted them. It was the first time I ever considered reaching out to God as an option because I didn't believe I had anything else. I didn't have anyone that could stop the monster in our house or the one emerging inside of me.

———————

Having a twisted sense of what was important evolved from my father's constant communication and reviling behavior towards me. Alcohol and his own history prevented him from becoming the man I believed he wanted to be because there were good things about him. There were times I could see that he tried because we did a lot of things as a family. I can't say I went without any material things because I had practically everything any kid could want including a drum set, BMX bike, motorcycle and all kinds of cool toys. My room should have been a sanctuary, however, there were too many beatings that took place inside those four walls causing excruciating recollections to echo in my head when I was alone. I just wish I were able to tell my father how I felt, maybe then, he would have made an effort to change.

Regardless of whether or not my father deserved it, I felt sorry for him. In a strange way, which I didn't entirely understand, I still loved him, but I was beginning to hate myself. He taught me how to ride a bike, shoot a gun, lie out of fear of him, and believe nothing I could do was good enough. Consequently, just to dispel his premeditated cynical judgments, I'd lie to make him proud of me, if even for a brief period. And seeing Mom smile made me believe the lie was worth it.

My father was incredibly handsome, resembling Robert Redford. When Dad raced his motorcycles I was in awe; I think we all were. In spite of the relationship I had with my father, I wanted to believe there was some sort of connection between us. I'd watch him on the dirt track with a great view from turn four. It was like watching the end of a football game when the score is tied and they're fighting with everything they have. If the motorcycles were to crash, I was out of luck because they'd head straight towards me. The only thing separating me from the track was a short cyclone fence that went up to my chin. I didn't care because I wanted to be as close to the race as I could. When the race began, Dad accelerated as hard as he could without getting any wheel spin. I'd watch him fearlessly rip around the track at full speed, slipstreaming past the other racers when he came off the turn. Waiting for him to surge out in front of everyone nearly suspended my breath until the race was over. Afterwards, my face would be covered with a film of dirt and it felt good.

The racetrack was the place I'd watch my father discharge his deep passion with extraordinary skill and meticulous timing. Sitting on his motorcycle appeared to dissipate whatever inner turmoil he had. The feeling that came over me as he crossed the finish line was something I never wanted to forget. I'd jump up screaming and hollering just like everyone else. The pride and admiration that a son wants to have for his father rose out of me more freely than I would have imagined possible. Anything good in me ascended to the surface. During those races, the man people cheered for was the father I prayed for. I tightly clung to those images as if they could save me from hating him, and perhaps in some unknown way, they did. He was the one I was proud of and loved, not the monster that followed him home.

If you allow the intrusion there's always someone that will work to cause a state of unrest in your life because that's what they're in. Naturally, in order for them to have some sort of relief, they inflict it upon others. I couldn't quite understand my father's methodology for doing things and my ability to block it out remained ineffective. Following one of his episodes, I closed my bedroom door and tried to release my anger by screaming, but it wouldn't come out. It stayed lodged inside and continued hurting me as though that was precisely where it belonged.

When Dad gave me chores, I was diligent in doing them, and he paid me well. It seemed I was never without having money. After mowing the lawn, cleaning the house, or doing whatever he allocated, his generosity followed. Being able to determine his way of thinking was impossible. I don't know if it was his way of apologizing for his anger or because I'd done the work properly. I never knew what was in his head so I just took what he paid me and thanked him. There were times that I did the chores the same way as always and he'd find something to be disgruntled about. Slowly, I was learning not to buy into it and just correct whatever issue he found.

I didn't think anyone evaluated the smoke-filled house along with the secrets and pain that it held. I allowed my environment to shape me into something I couldn't explain and it wasn't good. I couldn't understand how Troy and Kelly were able to escape it, but every situation, good or bad, affects people differently. Besides, I didn't know what they internalized, if anything. How we handle adversity is determined by more than one factor and no one really knows what that will be.

Time went on, desperation filled my mind, and darkness coursed through my veins making sure I knew my journey wasn't going to be easy.

———————

In the sixth grade something dark was threading inside of me like a web. Things began to resonate more clearly although I didn't fully understand the dynamics ahead of me. At the time, Troy was in college while Kelly traveled from Milan to New York to model. Like Mom, Kelly was absolutely beautiful.

As for my mother, she was stunning and could turn heads anywhere she went. She had a lethal combination of incredible intellect and unwavering drive. Mom played tennis, softball, and coached Kelly in just about everything. Mom always said they were a brutal pair when it came to tennis, and they were. I always believed my mother could accomplish anything she wanted because it was impossible to disconnect her from God. But I never understood why she was with Dad. There were times that they appeared to be really good together, but when it was bad, nothing should have kept her there. Perhaps it was for us, her children, or for me since I was the youngest. All I can say is that she stayed longer than our health could handle.

I couldn't take the blows upside my head and beatings with his belt. I had a generous amount of hatred for the life I was living and I wanted out. After several more years, death continued to summon me but I was still a coward. I'd been trying to stab myself since the third grade and it hadn't worked because I was still afraid. I continued absorbing the hate and randomly accepting the love until something ignited my father's fire again and again. I tried to let it go and shake it off but it happened too frequently, reminding me that I was despised.

My father always said I was stupid so when I finally accepted his label and everything he believed me to be, it felt liberating. I thought, perhaps then–*I'd no longer fall.*

The Fall

Four
The Bridge

Playing with my friends offered a necessary distraction in my life. It was unfortunate how quickly reality worked its way back when it was time to go home. Once our house was narrowly in sight, selfishly, reality managed to produce agonizing physical pain along with it. This time, I had a great deal filtering through my head so I took the longest route home.

When I reached the bridge, I imagined it would take me to a mythical place leading to something better. If I crossed it, I had to make it past the fiery pit of hell. I took a deep breath and stood motionless as if I were in a trance, reflecting on my life. I thought about Mom, Troy, Kelly, and Dad then wondered what was wrong with me. I looked down to find my wrists subconsciously rotating. I felt disconnected from what my life should have been. *And it should not have been like that.* My eyes watered because I didn't want to go through that day after day.

Most of my friends thought I was this fun kid that had the cool toys and a great life. Only it was far from the truth. I was loved and hated, beaten and hugged all in the same house. I was tired of hurting and the depression was too grueling to carry any further. Drained from not understanding what I did to deserve any of it, I discovered hiding the pain wasn't the solution nor was it worth it. Nothing was anymore.

I developed an extrinsic aspiration to die that had silently shattered me over the years. When my pain hit an excruciating altitude, I didn't want to go down a little at a time; I was ready to descend in flames. Mom tried to stop it, and I felt horrible for my lack of effort, but she couldn't see that I was living inside of my own prison just as I believed she was. In spite of it, she wanted to hold me to higher standards in life and in faith, but I had long lost the willingness to try. Initially, I felt guilty for doing so, but I believed there was no turning back.

People that loved me were disappointed in me because of my actions. What they didn't know was their disappointment made it easier for me to continue falling. We all handle stress, pain and loneliness in different ways, even if we live in the same house. It's forgotten that we're individuals with individual thoughts, feelings, comprehension and degrees of pain, which are nurtured by our surroundings. *Besides, I was a child.* After such a long continuum, my cries for help had fallen on deaf ears and this was the only way I knew how to flaunt the fallout. Yet, I never considered that it was impossible

The Bridge

for anyone to fix what he or she didn't fully understand.

The bridge was symbolic and poetic at the same time, which is why I believed it would be the ideal place. It had been calling me for years but I wasn't ready. Like one of those bridges in a movie, it was rustic, historic, magical, dangerous and open to interpretation. I was on a quest for peace and when I left the house, I found it. The air was unsullied and liberating, not toxic. Rather than the rise of disparaging darkness, daylight illuminated the sky. The branches of tall, abundant trees shaded the bridge instead of leaving it exposed to the scorching sun.

After stealing a deep breath, I headed unto the bridge willing to surrender. Instead of crossing it, I held on to the outside rail and crept sideways along it taking one step at a time. I recalled the many occasions my friends cried and yelled for me to stop playing around and come back on the bridge, but I couldn't. Each time I crossed the bridge, I was checking to see if that was the day.

The drop was precipitous and the downstream flow coursed faster than normal. I found the soft percolating of water gliding over and between the rocks pleasantly serene. The clear water displayed a colorful collection of little stones and large rocks that were everywhere as if they'd been strategically placed for the set of a movie. When I was trying to hide from my life I'd taken the challenging hike through tall grass to the bottom. I noticed the sun piercing gleefully through the trees that majestically lined the stream while I took in the fresh air, birds, squirrels and everything in sight. The rough bark on the oak trees and fast growing purple and yellow weeds below didn't escape me.

Admiring the craftsmanship of the bridge, I paused when I reached halfway, carelessly hanging on. My courage was intact and it was finally time to let go of that life. No one could fix it and I no longer had the aspiration to suffer in it as Todd James Myers. After years of pain and fear, I was tired of being part of the walking dead. To avoid being a coward, I returned to my imagination. Followed by a long serene breath, I opened my hands and took the fall into the fiery pit below *like lightning from heaven*, not having a single regret.

"I'm done."

Five
Trick Bag

I woke up taking a fast, deep breath as if I was coming up for air. In a panic, I began patting my chest with both hands to make sure I was alive. Then I patted my pockets, looking for my pipe.

"What the–where's my pipe?"

"Relax, Trick Bag. It's–look, it's right here. I just borrowed a few hits. You were out of it so–"

"So don't touch my shit! Wait! How do you *borrow* a few fuckin' hits?"

"Okay, okay man. Relax," he replied, staring at me with his dead eyes and dry, flaky skin trying to remember what he wanted to tell me.

"Umm, your–, your–," he grunted unintelligibly, scratching his dirty and disheveled brunette head of hair. Becoming impatient with his lack of logical communication, I stared at his mouth as if I could pull the words out. I noticed his cracked and parched lips were barely hiding his meth mouth of fractured, decayed and lost teeth. His drawn, sweaty face was covered with deep-pitted scars from scratching and picking. And his eyes were so heavily surrounded by dark circles, they may as well have been closed. Jimmy hadn't slept in days. Then he pointed at me; his mouth kept opening and shutting, revealing his complete loss of brain cells while he repeatedly took three steps back and then three steps forward lost in space and time. He looked like a puppet.

"What? What? What?" I snapped, reaching into my pocket like I had the last piece of gum hidden away. I pulled out a green Bic lighter and struck it several times creating useless sparks. It hurled what was left of my mind back to my childhood when I attempted to light a dry field of grass on fire to release the anger inside of me. But it didn't light. Since the lighter was out of fluid, with rising fury, I flung it across the dirty floor.

Jimmy kept scratching his head, as if that were somehow going to jog his faulty memory, repeating the same phrase, "Umm, your–, your–," but my patience were already adrift. I was tired of waking up after having the same reoccurring nightmare about my death, falling from *the bridge when I was a child*. It happened, and this was the life I chose.

I got up from the worn and malodorous chair to find a lighter that worked, when my pager vibrated. I snatched it off my waist and glanced at the number. It was him again. Only one person had that pager number and when he hit 666 he was reaching into the darkness for answers. He wanted something he wasn't willing to get himself and he needed someone to crawl around in the underbelly of the city to help him find it. I grabbed my ball cap and stumbled down the stairs with Jimmy yelling behind me, "Your–your pager keeps goin' off Trick Bag!"

"Really man?" I held the pager up so he could hear that it was still vibrating.

I only had a few minutes to make my way to a phone and today wasn't the day to search for one. When I stepped outside, I remembered seeing a booth by the corner store. Sheets of rain were falling like miniature darts underneath a grey and black sky leaving enough light to irritate my eyes. I'd been in the dark for a while. Seventeen years to be exact. It's what I preferred because it slid through my veins like escaping vapor. I grabbed the brim of my blue cap and made adjustments before tossing my hood over the top of it. Without calculating my route, I made a sloppy run to the corner hitting every puddle in my path. When I reached the phone booth, I snatched it off the receiver as the wrath of thunder made its presence known. I dug in my pocket, pulled out some change and quickly slipped it into the slot. Glancing at my pager to find the number, I let out a stressful sigh. Although I had to return his call daily, I hadn't committed it to memory. Perhaps I was hoping that part of my life would soon end so I could forget the number and him. I dialed before I ran out of time since there were consequences if I was late.

"You're pushin' it."

"No, see I had to get to a phone. I'm not at home and you know I don't have one. It's raining like crazy out here and–"

"And *you* know I don't give a damn. I didn't page you to listen to bullshit excuses. I need information. That's all I want from you!"

"It doesn't hurt to be cordial."

The Fall

"I heard there's somethin' you wanna tell me?"

I pulled the phone away from my face and looked at it in disbelief. This guy never stopped with his games.

"Tell you what? I don't know what you're talkin' about. Can you give me a clue or somethin'?" I asked, scratching my left arm. It was time for another hit and he was keeping me from it. Out of the corner of my eye, I noticed a guy slowly approaching me. He stopped and leaned against the brick building, making me feel uncomfortable. For all I knew, he could have been one of the Reaper's people trying to find out who I was giving information to. Maybe he was going to rob me, I didn't know. I covered the phone so he could see I was attempting to have a private conversation, but he didn't care. He stared at me like he had a problem. "Hold on," I said to Branson.

"Don't put me on hold!" he shouted back. But his ass was going on hold.

I turned to the guy and asked him, "What? What the fuck do you want? You see me on the fuckin' phone in the mother-fuckin'-rain, tryin' to have a conversation! Have some respect!"

"What's your problem, bro?" he said under his breath, as he turned to walk away.

"What the hell was that about?"

"Now you care? Like I said before all that shit, I don't know what the hell you're talkin' about."

"That's where you're wrong. I heard there were massive quantities of drugs and weapons brought in by some new players. To my understanding, they arrived last week, which you failed to mention."

"I can't tell you what I don't know and you seem to know more than me."

"You know more than you let on Trick Bag. You couldn't survive the streets in your current condition without knowing, smartass."

"Come on, massive quantities and weapons? You know I don't fuck with that set. They'd kill me because *they're killers!*"

"See, that's what I'm talkin' about. You do know more than you care to disclose. I suggest you find out who's movin' drugs through this city in the next twenty-four hours. If you can't figure it out, you're no use to me. Don't forget about the contract I have locked in the safe. Maybe I need to send you on a vacation. Yeah, I know the perfect spot for you. It overlooks the north side of the San Francisco Bay. It's uh–San Quentin. You've heard of it, right? At any rate, a little time there will help you remember more."

"I don't know why you keep threatening me."

"You don't?"

"No, I don't!"

"You know what? Let's make this simple. You're gonna do this for me because if you don't, you'll fuckin' end up with a bullet in your head! I'd be doin' you and your family a favor!"

"Just–just give me some time and I'll find out."

"Twenty-four hours." Click! He was gone.

I slammed the phone down. Clenching my teeth together out of anger, I said, "They think I'm gonna to be their informant, but I'm nobody's rat bitch! Period."

The only reason I even spoke to Branson was because I needed to keep my foot in the game to protect my family on the streets and stay out of prison. I scurried inside the corner store to buy a can of chew and a lighter before stumbling back down the street. I needed to function so I returned to the house I'd just left. Afterwards, I'd figure something out to keep the cops busy.

———————

A couple hours later I was back home. I wouldn't go beyond two days without talking to Mom. I picked up the phone on the counter and dialed her number. I smiled like nothing else mattered when she answered on the second ring.

"Mom?"

"Are you okay, sweetie?"

"Yeah, I'm fine," I lied.

After a brief moment of silence, she added sadly, "Honey–I don't get it."

"I know you don't."

"Thanks for letting me know you're okay. I love you, sweetheart."

"I love you too, Mama."

My heart sank immediately after hanging up. I had to regroup so I could get to work. Branson's demand made it possible for me to be dead in the next twenty-two hours. Interfering in someone's criminal activity wasn't advised. I was placing myself in a more unfavorable situation than I was already in.

"Detective got you running again?"

"I won't be long."

"That's what you always say."

Rosalyn didn't like the situation, but she accepted it for what it was. I could see in her eyes that she wanted to say something more. However, she knew it wouldn't change anything so she remained silent.

Trick Bag

What had I gotten myself into? What kind of life was this? Despite what anyone else saw, at least Mom knew the hell that trailed closely behind me since I was a child. I didn't know what my fate was but I knew she loved me and that was enough.

I went out to the shed, grabbed a few homemade items for bargaining, and headed back to the streets.

The Fall

Six
Effortless

Plodding through the gutter as long as I had
taught me how to be resourceful. If I wanted
information, all I had to do was ask. The skill was in
knowing the right people and how to retrieve the
information without making them think I needed it.
Casual conversation always worked. I'd give them a
little information and they gave me more or filled in
the missing pieces. I used it as my bargaining tool.
Like anyone in my position, I understood the game
because it's how I made my money. They were my
connections and I wasn't selling them out to save
myself. I was already lost.

Branson was tough and didn't make any
mistakes communicating what he was after. There
were major drug rings infiltrating the bay areas and
it was their job to stop them. Hell, that wasn't news.

The Fall

They'd been expanding for some time and their presence was notable. Drugs were becoming more widespread and being used to claim young teenage girls for dual purposes. The cops knew exactly what I was into, but they didn't want to stop me because I was too small for their massive problem. Whatever they were trying to find wasn't my business, and I didn't need more problems; I had enough of my own.

There was a lot happening in the city. If the cops did their job, they'd find what they were searching for just like I could. After spending the majority of my day in the streets, I'd go make a purchase and acquire free information along with it. I knew more than I cared to but I wasn't going to pick up the phone and call them.

One of the dealers I'd been introduced to had a clandestine lab on the outskirts of the Bay Area. He moved around to keep from being located, but when he wanted to be found he could. Whenever I stopped by his spot I could tell he'd been working and building his business. Being handsome and well-groomed definitely came into play for making introductions. He had an infallible system for canvassing the streets to solicit young girls to work for him. His tactics were seductive and invitational rather than intimidating. Nearly every time I saw him, he had a new girl that was young and attractive. It didn't take long before they were strung out with their youth ripped from them. People think these girls end up on the street because of a drug habit,

which isn't entirely true. The streets are full of
veteran predators. He'd meet them out somewhere
hanging with their friends in the most unsuspecting
places. Being crafty, he'd casually strike up an
engaging conversation to make them comfortable
enough to accept his invitation to hang out. He
claimed there was always that one risk taker in a
group of *good girls* who wanted to be exploratory,
feeling she was a little different than the others. He
could spot her the same way he could an opportunity
to set up a lab and it was all business from there. His
targets were those who were broken, lonely, or risk
takers.

He called it *effortless.* Effortless for him perhaps,
but I believed that someone else put the work in to
break his targets before they ever reached him. He
said he'd start them off with harmless small talk and
a stiff drink. It worked. At that age, they will only see
what is consciously desired. If they haven't been
taught, with conviction, not to believe everything
they hear, they may. Before the end of the night the
girls were persuaded, loose, and intoxicatingly at
ease. He didn't push or reveal his dark side until the
other girls were gone, leaving their friend, the risk
taker, behind. And if by chance the risk taker left with
her friends that time, he'd say, "It doesn't matter,
she'll be back."

Once she did, he'd give her a few drinks with
ecstasy and introduce her to her first hit of a glass
pipe, containing a potent dose of her new addiction.
With a steely grin, he'd convince her that it was
harmless, and she'd want to believe him. After the
pipe touched her innocent pink lips, it was over. He
had another fresh recruit for any purpose he desired.
The girls didn't see it coming and that's why they

took the fall. After the mind is altered for a period of time, the physical changes follow.

The problem is typically concealed for so long that by the time it's discovered, the choices are death by addiction or life through rehab. These are the type of choices no one should have to make.

Parents want to believe that they know how to protect their children. Considering what I've seen, they should think again. The same way my parents didn't tell me everything, I definitely didn't offer them the whole truth. Parents have to accept the reality of how children learn to hide their life. Fear of disappointment is only a small part of the reason; the other is through observational learning.

It may be difficult for some to articulate, but we don't want parents in our business, judging our young indiscretions or tempering the mounting arrogance. At a certain point, we may choose to craft a life where it becomes liberating to answer to no one. However, when we fall, we fall into the abyss and sometimes the only one that can reach us is God.

Parents often say they trust their kids, but they should consider they are entrusting them to *everything* outside of their grasp. The claws that grab them are razor-sharp and undeniably fatal. When kids leave their home, parents are typically more comfortable if they're with their friends. They think safety in numbers is the key, but not always. If those numbers have *one* risk taker in the bunch or someone that's going through a rough time, it's likely for them to become a target to dealers, sex traffickers, or anyone wanting to destroy a life for their own gain. Let's not forget the other kids are in jeopardy because of the association. The funny thing is that we forget, "In God we trust"-*not man.* Those girls emerged and vanished at his hands and no one ever knew the cause or origin of the problem. It was business to him, but intended rebellion or fun to the girls. It happens more than people want to believe and many of these children die because of it. Imagine how many secrets children keep from their parents and then give consideration to the massive secrets small towns possess. The reason they're successful masking its dirty indiscretions is because there isn't enough law enforcement or hours in the day to stop it. Many of those indiscretions or secrets are deadly.

For a few difficult years, I worked, played, and aimlessly wandered in the streets taking notice of everything possible. The longer you stay there, the more you become it or die observing the death of others until it's your turn. When the sky transitioned to black, things transpired that weren't remotely close to being conceivable to the human mind. When that has become your world, they don't escape you.

I knew I was pretty damaged to dwell in the streets instead of fighting to get my life back. Nevertheless, when you've fallen so far, it's easier to pick up momentum and keep falling. I didn't force myself to climb out of that life while I was still on a respirator, I stayed down. The penalty was nearly two lost decades before I admitted to being adrift and beaten down from that way of life. I became accustomed to its acquired taste. After making the choice to exist that way, I was afraid there wasn't anyone that could help me. No one was to blame for where I was at that point because there were other paths I could have taken.

My life was a mess, but it was difficult for me to see homeless or hooked girls on the street. I believed they could have been anything they wanted. Knowing

The Fall

what they were facing made me sick, because I was cognizant of what my own life entailed. My uncertainty became frightening.

Seven
High School

The unpleasantries I intentionally indulged in during high school weren't articulated to my parents. I kept everything hidden until it was too late or rather, glaringly evident by my behavior and dismissive attitude. Concealing the truth made it impossible for them to safeguard me. I stayed away from home and with friends as much as possible or hid in the confines of my room. And when the storm came, its downpour washed away the line between responsible and irresponsible.

Most days, I was actually high in high school. In fact, I recall smoking weed for the first time in my life in a bathroom stall. I was supposed to be in auto shop during that time but instead, I made the choice to try it. I can't remember laughing that much since I was a child. It didn't take long before I was sprawled out on the bathroom floor gripping my stomach as tightly as I could just to minimize the pain from laughing so hard. Streams of tears liberally rolled down my cheeks. It must have been built up and when it came out, I'd never felt so free. Within a week, I bought an ounce of weed and my habit began.

Shrouded with anger and pain, my arrogance kept me from foreseeing the deception I allocated would ultimately be to my detriment. No longer was I regulated or in harmony with the natural flow of life.

By twelfth grade, the damage was complete and I did more than dabble in drugs; I sold them. I did anything I felt like doing, believing it would discharge my pain, like Tony Montana. Once the gravitational pull drew me into its circumference, I ventured closer to the central part of it. My impervious effort to self-destruct rendered me unmanageable, but quite popular with the wrong crowd.

During my senior year, there were seven periods and each class counted as one cut if I ditched class. My girlfriend was almost twenty and already out of high school so I spent most of my days at her house when her parents were gone. I had incurred two hundred and thirty seven cuts by May, which caused me to be kicked out of high school a month before graduation. My grades were good enough for me to graduate had I remained focused, but I chose the girl over school.

In an attempt to keep me motivated so I would graduate, Mom enrolled me in another high school but it didn't feel right because I was already eighteen. I was embarrassed by the choices, which caused me to leave. I didn't consider what it would do to Mom if I didn't graduate but afterwards, I could sense the disappointment. However, the desire to graduate hadn't evaded me and I knew that I needed to acquire my GED, so I got it.

Mom wasn't aware that I'd already committed to the life I'd chosen, although I was ignorant to what I was soliciting. Still, I was relentless and moved forward. Going deeper didn't scare me. My curiosity enhanced my innate hunger for it because the thought of *the fall caused me to lose fear.* Once I tasted the bitterness of the dark side, I was certain I would lust after it for the rest of my life.

I didn't see myself on the other end of the spectrum because I hadn't considered what the landscape would contain. Vomiting, deception, meth cravings, pain, death threats, homelessness, and everything I didn't want was what I had. I didn't predict any of it because I only cared about what I was doing at that moment and nothing else.

The Fall

Eight
Back in Black

It was late one summer night and I'd been running the streets for a few days before I crossed paths with a girl from my past. Kaleigh was the baby sister of Ross, one of my closest friends since elementary school. Their father passed away shortly after she was born. However, they both appeared to be happy and considerably close with their Mom until cancer claimed her when Kaleigh was a senior in high school.

Ross and Kaleigh were inseparable and it was obvious that she idolized her big brother. Everyone loved Ross because he was the guy that resolved conflicts instead of instigating them. In high school, he was a solid athlete and an all around fun guy. He always wore a Giants ball cap pulled snuggly over his thick brown hair. When we played baseball, Kaleigh would sit in the grass Indian style with her little friends and cheer for her brother. When we hung out, she was sure to tag along whenever she could. I was almost twenty-eight when Ross was killed in a car accident. He was on-duty at the time. Someone rammed into his car, causing it to spin out of control and collide with a big oak tree. Ross was killed upon impact and they never caught who did it. Kaleigh was beginning graduate school at the time. As anyone would have expected, the death of her only brother shredded her whole world. When I saw her at the funeral, her blank expression surrounding her red, puffy eyes broke me even more. I was trying to hold it together just so I could approach her, but it was obvious that she was too.

After handling some of her brother's affairs, Kaleigh told me she was returning to school. But for some reason, she never left. No one really understood why because there was nothing for her in Pleasanton other than heartache.

A couple years later, I was shocked to find her staggering down the broken cements steps of a known dealer's dilapidated dwelling. When she hit the sidewalk, she stumbled into me and muttered something indistinct. In an attempt to understand her, without appearing threatening, I delicately lifted her frail chin with the tips of my fingers and stared directly at her mouth while she spoke. Trying to reconstruct the girl I once knew, my eyes instinctively traced the details of the shattered innocence on her face. It seemed as if she was doing the same thing with me.

"Todd, right?"

"Yeah," I said letting go of her.

Back in Black

I realized I'd passed her a couple of times here and there but her hair was always draped in her face and she never made eye contact with me. Prior to that moment, I wouldn't have known it was Ross's kid sister until I recreated the vision of her. Rail thin with long, oily, red hair, Kaleigh wasn't older than twenty-five but she appeared to have suffered a rough thirty-five years. Looking beyond the austerity of her life, I was able to detect some semblance of beauty that was once visible in her jade eyes, but I don't think she could. She'd look away or hang her head when she spoke as though she'd been badly beaten. Her clothes were ragged and the sleeveless emerald blouse she had on revealed track marks on her arm. The blood, delicately tracing her right nostril, alluded to cocaine being another vice.

Kaleigh slowly elevated her voice to a detectable level as though she had something to confess, but she didn't offer anything other than the obvious.

"You probably don't remember me. Do you?"

"Yeah. Of course I do."

Her barren eyes gave a slight look of surprise. "Really?"

"You're Ross's kid sister." Once I realized that must have sounded insensitive, I quickly tried to put it another way. "I mean, Kaleigh, right?"

"Yup! It's me. Not the *me* you were probably expecting though."

"Huh?"

"I guess you're wondering what happened? College girl and all."

"I don't have the right to judge anyone. Isn't it obvious I'm having trouble with my own life?"

She dropped her head and whispered softly, "Maybe I'll–I'll see you around."

"Maybe," I shrugged.

I began walking away with a determined stride as if I had somewhere to go because it hurt me to see Kaleigh like that. I glanced over my shoulder and noticed her sloppily trailing behind me the same way she used to do with Ross. After a few yards, I slowed down so she could catch up. She continued making small talk and the more I replied, the more she spoke. It didn't take long before Kaleigh shared her story as we wandered through the streets of downtown Pleasanton. Tightly clutching her oversized hippie style bag, something told me it held all of her worldly belongings.

She tried to appear indifferent to the reality that she had nowhere to go. Only she wasn't. I saw a young girl that was terrified of what her life had become and it echoed the fate others had befallen. I'd been living that fate on my own accord, but she was lost. It wasn't difficult for me to look into her eyes and catch the reflection of myself before I became Trick Bag. I was certain she didn't want to exist that way either. Whatever promises were made in the streets were nothing more than lies that the streets told. That life wasn't better. It's where you go to become invisible until you die. No one expects anything of you and when they give up on believing you can possibly change, it's over. That's when you know *this is it* until you decide it isn't.

We walked over to the park and sat on a wooden bench. I felt as though she'd been holding it all in. Kaleigh had a lot to say but she said no one ever cared. Why would they? But at that moment, I did. I always tried to give people what I wanted. Even then, I needed someone to hear me, but that wasn't possible because I ran everyone away. All I could do was listen to Kaleigh and give her the opportunity to talk about whatever she wanted, and she did.

Kaleigh leaned back and stretched out her legs like she was looking up at the stars, only the clouds were obstructing the view. She started articulating her thoughts as if she were sharing a story in class that no one wanted to hear. Kaleigh believed that being an addict wasn't her fault, but I knew who possessed the power of that choice. She brushed her hair off of her shoulders and sighed as if she were about to tell me a secret. Nervously fidgeting with her dirty, jagged fingernails, she explained that regardless of what anyone thought, she needed the drugs to suppress the hate and pain she was forced to live with.

After the funeral, Kaleigh was at Ross's home packing up his belongings. Ross was pretty well-known so his death emitted a lingering sadness. That evening, two men broke into his house. Kaleigh said they appeared to be looking for something when she caught them off guard. She was badly beaten and raped. A big part of Kaleigh died that night which is the reason she didn't return to school. A warm body searching to bury the pain is what was left of Kaleigh. I felt her anguish and understood her death.

One week after another, she sat in Ross's house waiting for it to go away, like a nightmare, but it never did. When she finally ventured out, she began frequenting a bar; seeking a way to end the confined torment she carried. Eventually, she found what she called, "medicine".

Ross encouraged her to go away to college as a way of helping his sister salvage some sense of stability after their mother passed. His death inserted another layer she'd have to overcome. She knew Ross would want her to fight; only the cowards that brutally raped Kaleigh pushed her out of that world and into mine. One thing led to another; she began inhaling lines of white powder and graduated from there. It seemed to be a quick solution to alleviate suffering that would prove to be infinite. When it captured her soul, she took the fall and hadn't been able to recover from it since. The more I listened, the more my own narrative emerged.

Kaleigh was one of the five girls I'd gotten to know that housed some type of concentrated pain. They took the fall into a life where they tried not to feel anything. None of them were aware of the substantial price they'd pay, and it had the ability to turn deadly. When people get high off meth, cocaine, heroin, or other drugs for the first time, they think they will experience that same euphoric feeling again, but that's the lie. They'll keep trying to duplicate that sensation but will never achieve anything other than graduating to harder drugs. The frequency increases as their body becomes immune to the feeling. Out of desperation, they will continue searching for it. That first euphoric feeling is actually the last. Everything else is nothing more than the vile addiction.

I expected their stories to be vastly different but each of them had a common synopsis. Because they were young, they believed in the fallacy that the streets were better than home, or the place to remove pain. I was twenty-nine and *still* struggling out there too, but it bothered me to see Kaleigh having exposed herself to a death sentence. I wanted her to get up and find a way to fight so she could get her life back. I didn't want her to be me, if she lived that long. *I didn't want anyone to be me.*

Back in Black

Ominous colors suspended above whispered that midnight had come and gone. The trees swayed to their own melodic tune anticipating the downpour that would soon blanket the town. With hurried steps, we made our way over to a Laundromat for the night. We collapsed on the dirty tiled floor talking, until sleep claimed Kaleigh. The last thing I asked her was if she knew who raped her. She closed her eyes and incoherently uttered, "He was a big, big ugly snake with horns." I didn't get it. But it was a good thing I didn't, because if I did–

It was impossible for me to doze off on meth so I held her as she slept, curled up, like the child I remembered. I wanted to protect her and send her someplace safe, but I couldn't even help myself. *I leaned over and whispered in her ear.*

I thought about what I'd done to my life and if I had time to change it. I wondered if I could find the strength to become a better brother and son one day. Kaleigh made me accept the sad truth that this type of life wasn't exclusive to me or remotely close to where I belonged. I wasn't the only one that held my pain captive. There is more than *one* cause for people to give up on life, but the gift of life itself should be reason enough to fight. I needed to find the strength to fight before it was too late or had I already used my nine lives?

Disrupted by the violent crashing, I listened to the insanely rhythmic tapping against the roof and then returned to my childhood, reminiscing to *Back in Black.*

The Fall

Nine
New Beginnings

It was in the early hours of the morning when I pushed the curtain aside and peeked out my window. Dense fog hovered about intentionally obstructing my view. The sun hadn't begun to ascend. I wanted to return to the comfort of my bed, drag the blanket over my messy head of hair, and plunge into a lengthy slumber. Although I wasn't completely awake, I had to get dressed for school. I hadn't been feeling that well, which caused my movements to be rather sluggish. I sauntered across the hall into the bathroom, reached inside the shower, and turned the knob so the water could warm up. After slipping out of my blue and red plaid pajamas I pulled the shower curtain aside to step in. Interrupted by a powerful blow to the back of my head, I fell to my knees. While uncontrollably pissing all over the floor, I became aware of the belt in my father's hand. He exploded in a fit of rage savagely beating me until I crumbled. This time, it was because the noise from the shower woke him up. I cried out begging him to stop, but as the adrenaline surged through him, he applied more force with each strike. He didn't want to stop because my pain was giving him the release he needed. Trying to avoid the belt, I wedged myself between the tub and the toilet, and then I heard my mother's fast approaching footsteps. Mom raced into the bathroom yelling for my father to stop. Without hesitating, she began pounding on his back with closed fists trying to get him off of me. Making a swift turn, he used his body to back her out of the bathroom and against the hallway banister. With urine dripping from my naked body, I fought to stand then lunged at him, striking him repeatedly in the back. I couldn't defend myself, but there was no way I'd let him hurt my mother. This time, I was fighting to pull him off of her before the wobbling banister collapsed, but his strong arm shoved me away. I stumbled a few steps backwards and when he released her, Mom fell to her knees.

After realizing what he'd done or may have been capable of, he gave an icy stare while forcibly gritting his teeth. Petrified, I watched him walk through the heavy steam escaping the bathroom, and then the bedroom door slammed shut. I never felt more hated by him than at that moment. Mom and I huddled on the floor crying together until our tears subsided. I can't pinpoint the exact reason, but Mom hugged me in a way that made me certain she'd *never* allow that to happen again. "I'm sorry. I love you," Mom cried with tears staining her flushed face. When I got up and returned to the bathroom, the water was still running.

Over the next few weeks, I found it more difficult to concentrate in school. I was emotionally, spiritually, mentally and physically drained. Even when I was doing my schoolwork, I couldn't complete the tasks. The situation at home became worse and after what he did to me, he should have been doing time in jail.

Riding my bike to school in the eighth grade offered a welcomed emotional and psychological release. The path took fifteen miles on my BMX bike, which I road from the furthest point south of town. When I hit Main Street, the sidewalks had wooden boards that sounded like riding on a boardwalk. I'd make a left turn by Dean's Café, a popular little breakfast spot, and then follow the road all the way to Dublin. The majestic looking homes lining the perfectly landscaped street were built in the late 1800's. When I'd stop momentarily to look at the homes, I could only imagine what stories were created between those walls. I'd push off and continue on through Valley Trails. When I reached the bridge, I'd pause before crossing it. I viewed it as a mythical place that had some kind of power.

I rode on dirt trails and in the street but the excitement progressed when I reached a stoplight. As if I were my father racing his motorcycle, I'd glance both ways before zipping right through the red light to get a jumpstart. Some of the cars would hit on their gas and then leave me in the dust but I didn't care because it was a lot of fun. The best part was that I had the freedom to ride thirty miles round trip to school. I knew where all the jumps were and which squares on the sidewalk were raised up to launch me two or three feet in the air. I loved it!

By the end of September or beginning of October, the rain came in a bit more. There were times when Dad's friends would pass me riding my bike at the bottom of a hill. They'd usually wave or blow the horn but when it was pouring, they stopped to pick me up and put my bike in the trunk.

———————

I was awakened by heavy thunder and pouring rain thrashing against the rooftop, which meant Dad would take me to school that day. We left early to give him enough time to stop at Dean's Café. He was meeting Denny, a guy they recruited as a splicer for their company. After studying his features, it hit me, he reminded me of the actor, Sam Elliot. I was impressed by the way he spoke and enthralled by his charismatic nature so he had my full attention. It didn't take long before I wanted to emulate his characteristics. When kids are young, some are impressionable or looking for role models and for some reason, I felt he would fill that role. Denny wasn't a celebrity or a musician; he was just himself. Innately, I knew he would be in my life in some capacity.

The waitress came over and politely took our orders. The way Denny smiled made her light up. Familiar with the menu, I ordered The Classic, which consisted of two eggs over easy, bacon, country potatoes, an English muffin, and a large glass of orange juice. While they were discussing business, I picked at the food on my plate and listened in awe.

New Beginnings

Much like my father, Denny seemed fairly knowledgeable about their industry and I found him pretty observant. While Denny was asking questions, he'd continue to show regard to me by cutting his eyes in my direction or giving me an approving nod with a pleasant smile. I didn't appear to be invisible to him, which made me feel important. I was in the ninth grade, frail, and fearful of my father, but I wasn't afraid of Denny. I liked him.

As the weeks filed in, one after another, Denny came around a lot more. I was on the city league's baseball team, the Expos, and my sister's boyfriend, Mike, was one of the coaches. At that time, I was one of the smallest kids on the team. Denny began to show up to my practices like he was feeling me out, and then he started coming to my games. He'd watch the game, beat on his cigarette, wave, and then leave. It was something my father never did, which gave the impression that Denny cared. That alone pushed me to take my athletic ability to another level just to keep his attention.

Denny began to take more of a genuine interest in the dynamics of Mom, Dad and me, *the broken kid*, the way I wished my father had done. My father spent time with me, but not in the way Denny was beginning to invest his. At that age, there were more things I needed to learn from my father and Denny was trying to teach me some of those things. He articulated the purpose of having morals and courage by sharing relatable stories. Then, he explained the importance of being a good person, which was something I allowed to gradually escape my character. Through our conversations, Denny offered inspirational words that filled up an empty space I had inside of me. Soon, I started to feel conflicted because he wasn't my father. During that period, Dad was either working or out driving around in his red Ferrari 308 GTS.

Regardless of my mindset, Denny was there for me, but I noticed that he was starting to spend more time with Mom. I could see something building between them when I was sitting by the Xerox machine doing my homework in her office. The energy between them was nothing less than electric. By the look of things, there didn't seem to be any stopping those two. I slouched in the chair, peeked over my left shoulder, and smiled at the way they interacted. It gave me hope that it could happen between them.

My parent's relationship appeared to have reached the point that the best thing for my mother was a man that could give her something she didn't have. When there's something you desperately yearn for and someone unsuspectingly gives it to you without expecting anything in return, they become someone you trust, respect, and perhaps love. Denny recognized my need for a father figure and became that for me. The only problem is that his arrival was too late. The internal damage was progressively working its way through my system and I was taking on a life in the unknown.

When I was six, Mom asked my father to move out. Obviously, things weren't working between them. I could tell she tried to keep our family together, but even as a kid, I thought it was better that way. I felt warm and happy that he was gone because Mom always had music playing, we were able to eat what we wanted, sleep in on the weekends, and breathe comfortably in a relaxed environment. It was like our first vacation. We actually went out and got our first dog, Mittens, a little Lhasapoo.

.   Things couldn't have been better but just as the seasons returned, six months later, so did my father. He was on the front porch crying and begging my mother to take him back. He'd gotten a DUI and I think Mom felt sorry for him because she let him back in. Although he was on his best behavior for two years, the negative energy was gradually restored to our lives. It wasn't always that way, but I had many unmovable thoughts of unhappiness that eclipsed nearly everything good.

There were a lot of things I wanted to forget but being fourteen years old wasn't one of them. I remember the significant event that caused my airways to open and restored my ability to breathe without a struggle. I never had any doubt that Mom loved Dad, but I'm certain she was ready to ascend from the ocean floor and serenely breathe after their divorce. It wasn't an easy process for them and it was difficult for me. My mother was so broken that she wasn't capable of being there the way I needed her to be. Since Dad was gone, I thought I was going to get my mom back except she began dating Denny. When their relationship took off, something between Denny and I changed, which caused me to return to the chaotic pattern I'd already set in motion. My siblings had graduated high school making me the only kid at home. The dynamics made me feel slightly displaced again, but it wasn't Mom's fault, she deserved to be happy.

That year, Denny became my stepfather and Mom appeared to be genuinely happy. He was an endearing man who told passionate stories about

The Fall

Vietnam, as well as his time in Alaska and Saudi Arabia. His nickname was the Marlboro Man.

One of the things I loved was that Mom always had a grand vision and without it, none of what was created would be in existence. She built a successful skin care business and when she married Denny, she sold it to two of her girlfriends from high school.

Mom and Denny decided to start their own company by combining their strengths and using their expertise in the capacity beneficial to the company's development. They purchased a home with a warehouse in the back and Mom used the money from the sale of her company for the new one. They specialized in underground high-voltage cable installation, splicing, and terminating like she had done with Dad. Regardless of how busy they became or how hard they worked, nothing seemed to be more important to Mom than her relationship with God. She had a lot of responsibilities, but she never let anything distract her from God.

My father continued to run what was now his company down the street from Mom and Denny's, but he focused on making quick money. He and Mom had a different set of ethics.

Mom and Denny had their challenges in the beginning, but it appeared that she was able to focus with more clarity. She had a gift for looking at the big picture and I believe that helped her create a plan for her future. She was an impressive business owner and made tough decisions for the company, but in time, those choices made everyone closer. She believed that honesty and integrity would prevail. When it came to the business, her preference was to stay behind the scenes and make things happen. I

94

was happy to see my mother with someone that made her smile.

Denny worked hard running everything out in the field. Even though my time with Mom was limited, Denny was healthier for me than I think anyone realized because he pushed me to be better. My sister liked him too, but my brother remained close to Dad. I was grateful Denny came into our lives when he did because I felt he literally saved us. Only it didn't take long before I started sliding down the path I was already slated on.

Many of the people I met on the street had a home life equivalent to mine or worse. There were reasons our faith was broken and most of us had that common denominator. Faith has a lot to do with what can affect us and to what measure. If I hadn't forgotten what I was taught, I would have been stronger. I was easily affected and influenced because I was weak. It didn't take long for me to fall prey to the epidemic of substance abuse.

Typically, it's expected to make a few poor choices when you're young. The problem is when they don't wane. When I was twenty-three, I didn't take my actions under consideration the way I should have, but after years of partying and doing what felt good to me, it became a part of my character.

When Mom and Denny were in Hawaii, further establishing their company, I had access to their home to feed their dogs and water the plants. It should have been a sign that even with my history they continued to give me the benefit of learning to be more responsible. However, when I finished, I helped myself to the credit cards I found in a drawer. I wasn't thinking about any of the repercussions because I didn't care about anything other than myself. I took advantage of the situation because I could.

Twenty-five brought about an opportunity for me to settle down and let go of some of my long established habits. Light and darkness cannot coexist so I needed to release the darkness that was crammed inside of me. If I didn't, as long as I was alive, it would remain dormant with the threat of rising when it was time.

———————

I'd been in a serious relationship with a girl that had my heart since I was eighteen. We knew one another in a unique way and fit together beautifully. Although I was working, I sold weed to make extra money. Financially, we were doing well with an additional three to four thousand a week so we weren't without anything. Things between us seemed perfect and it made sense to get married.

A few years later, the marriage was no longer working for either of us, but it wasn't because she didn't try. I couldn't communicate what was happening so I just let it run its course. After we divorced, nothing seemed to be the same.

Like Mom, Denny wanted me to work harder to get my life back on track because they saw my transformation. Given the choices I'd made and the effort Denny put into trying to save me from myself, I disappointed him and continued to work towards becoming exactly what he feared.

New Beginnings

Denny tried to alter my decision as to which route I'd take through life by giving me what parental guidance he could offer. He saw the warnings and perhaps it was easier to detect as an outsider, nonetheless, Denny was powerless over my history. I needed to get better and since nothing else worked, perhaps my journey was necessary. Only God knew when and how it would end.

I caused an uncomfortable division between Denny and me because of the choices I made, not only in my personal life, but in business. I regretted it because Denny loved me and it was apparent that I'd hurt him, just as I had everyone else. My skin wasn't thick enough to keep his disappointment away from my heart.

The Fall

Ten
A Familiar Hiding Place

My day had been quite uneventful. It slipped away like melting ice on the cement as the sun began to wearily descend. I was hoping that the temperatures would too. It was the beginning of September in 1999 and I was sitting contentedly on my sofa talking with a couple of friends. Throughout my years of selling weed, I'd met a lot of people that stopped over to buy, get high, hang out or play Madden because there wasn't much else to do in my mental state other than play basketball, which I loved.

Jeremy was one of the guys that hung out at my place on a regular basis. When I was a young, he lived in the neighborhood and we often played ball on opposing teams. We weren't close because he always seemed to have a hidden agenda or lurking vengefulness. As the years went by, things changed when we started getting high together. To pass time, we'd reminisce about some of the football games we played as kids.

My parents bought a house down the street from a beautifully manicured open field. When I was eight years old, I enjoyed when my friends and I gathered there to engage in brutal games of tackle football. We played a lot of good games, but one in particular stayed etched in my memory as the best of them all.

After playing for a couple of hours, the game was tied. We only had one more play before we were out of time. To make it worse, their quarterback threw an extraordinary Hail Mary pass to his receiver. I sprinted after their receiver with everything I had in me but it looked doubtful that he'd miss the pass. With nothing to lose, I turned my body perfectly in sync with the receiver, leapt into the air, picked it off, and ran it back for a touchdown! We won! The guys were jumping around, full of excitement.

Their quarterback came over, patted me on the shoulder and asked, "How did you do that?"

"I don't know," I told him. "I guess when someone wins, someone has to lose and I didn't want it to be us."

The receiver was Jeremy. I could tell the story still bothered him, only it was told in fun. That was decades ago.

While sharing that little piece of history, I happened to get up from my comfortable seat on the sofa to grab my bottle of Jack Daniels from the kitchen. Inadvertently, through the narrowly open blinds, I caught sight of a fully armed tactical unit coming up the long walkway towards my house with a battering ram in tow. They were about to break the door down and raid my place!

"Shit!" I said locking my hands together on top of my head. I paced the floor trying to determine a counter move.

"Bro, what's wrong?" Jeremy asked, noticing a drastic change in my demeanor. He got up and headed towards the window to see what I was freaking out over.

"Don't touch the blinds! Cops! They're headed this way!" I replied nodding at the door.

"What for?"

"Warrants."

"What do I do, Trick Bag?"

"Don't answer! And get rid of the–"

"I got you. Just go! Get outta here!" he said, grabbing a glass pipe and meth off the table.

"I don't want any part of this," Jeremy's girlfriend mumbled from the kitchen before continuing to puff on her cigarette like she was half asleep.

Shelby was hardly able to talk, let alone, move. Ignoring her, I pushed both parts of the brown sectional against the front door and disappeared into the back bedroom.

I could see five or six squad cars blocking the parking area with their blue and red lights flashing. While they were doing the standard knocking and announcing, I planned on making good use of those fifteen to twenty seconds. I slid open the window, popped the screen out, climbed up on the ledge, and jumped from the second story. I crashed against the concrete patio and fumbled to get up. The wooden gate to the fence was padlocked so I climbed over it and scampered across the parking lot towards the stream.

A cyclone fence, approximately eight feet high, partitioned off the stream from the property. I looked over my shoulder and saw a cop turning the corner. As soon as I leapt onto the fence I heard, "There he is!" Convinced he'd fire if he had the shot, I jumped to the other side, ripping a chunk of flesh off my left shin. While blood dripped down my leg, adrenaline hurled me in that fight or flight response and I hightailed it down the hill, fleeing alongside the edge of the stream. With dogs barking behind me, I ran like I was in that football game with Jeremy all over again. The cops were forced to go around the fence with the dogs, giving me a decent start. I kept running with *everything I had in me.*

I'd given Branson bad information to redirect his focus. Okay, so he was upset. Only I wasn't ready to go to jail. I was tired of being used and bullied so I fled.

Covered with sweat, gasping for air, and scared, I ran as far as I could before they'd have me in sight again. I trudged through the cool water to wash off my scent, but I needed a hiding place. When I lifted my head, as if I were waiting for an answer, I saw the bridge, and it hit me. I crouched down, laid in the stream and folded my arms across my chest, allowing the water to sheathe me, like the lid of a coffin.

The barking subsided and it seemed I had eluded them that time. I waited until I could no longer hold my breath and I came up for air. They were gone. Soaked and shivering, I ran to a payphone and called my mother.

"Mom!"

"Todd. Where are you, sweetheart? What's wrong?"

"Mom, they didn't get me. I'm okay–" I reassured her, beginning at the end of the story.

———————

When I was nine, my father bought me a black kingsnake and he built a cage for me to keep it in. The cage sat on my dresser, but being elusive, Lusi escaped. When I came home from playing with friends that Sunday afternoon, Mom wasn't pleased. She informed me that my snake was *somewhere* in the house. She wanted it captured and taken out so it wouldn't happen again. Two hours later, like a lamppost, I found it upright in a corner of the living room. Dad advised me to take Lusi down by the stream and let it go.

I tied the cage on the back of my bike and took my pet snake to the stream. I parked my bike, removed the cage and carried it down the hill towards the water. I had a hard time releasing something I loved into an unfamiliar place, especially during the winter when the temperatures dipped to nearly twenty degrees. I didn't know where Lusi would live so it took a few hours before I could open the cage. I sat on the grass having flashbacks of my life. With each aching memory I sobbed harder and harder until there was nothing left.

I reached over and slowly raised the lid to the cage allowing Lusi to slither out. The only boundaries would be nature. I hoped that Lusi could create a better life than I had. Disheartened, I left and returned home.

That night, sleeping was difficult because I wondered if my snake was safe, scared, or hurt. The next day, after school, I hopped on my bike and returned to the stream to find Lusi. I went down the hill and found the cage exactly where I left it. The lid was open, so I looked inside to find Lusi coiled up like a cinnamon roll. Having lived only in captivity, my snake didn't know how to avoid the perils of nature and froze to death.

Although the tactical unit couldn't apprehend me that day I fled to the stream, eventually, Branson kept his promise. A few weeks later, they arrested me while I was headed to see Hank. I went to jail for driving on a suspended license, drug possession, and possession of drug paraphernalia. I'd grown accustomed to his threats, which alleviated the fear of jail. I wasn't doing anything to keep me locked up long enough, and Branson didn't like it. As soon as I got out, he'd show up again. Playing Branson's informant wasn't an option unless I went to rehab and put the work in. As long as I chose to live that way, I gave Branson authority over me.

I was tired of being chased, caught, high, lonely, confused and afraid to ask God to help me. I needed to get my life together. I didn't have much of a relationship with my brother or sister because I wasn't relatable anymore and I probably hadn't been for years. When I wasn't feeling sorry for myself, I wondered what gave me the right to judge my father for his actions given who I was. Others fought to have normalcy and happiness in their life, which made it difficult for them to accept what I was choosing to do with mine.

I made my way through the motions of rehab hoping *it* could fix me only it doesn't work that way. Rehab is where I had to commit to fixing myself while respecting and following their guidance without any excuses.

At one point, I went in and out of rehab three different times in five days. I wanted a quick fix to get better, which was the same reason I used drugs. And after decades of complaining about the same incidents, history has the tendency to validate reasons of self-pity. Besides, I didn't believe it was possible for me to recover from over a decade of drug abuse after having brief stints of sobriety. On one occasion, I was actually making an effort and I felt good about it. It bothered me that it was winter and there were people across the street in the park that didn't have the capacity to stay warm. I grabbed all of the blankets I could find around the facility and took them outside to the homeless. I knew I was breaking their rules; nevertheless, I believed it was the right thing to do. I was kicked out of rehab but that time, I thought it was worth it!

If it weren't for my mother paying for me to live in hotels when I didn't have a place to stay, I would have been in a worse situation and that could have been me. Regardless of what I was going through, she wanted me to have a warm place to go. Although I wasn't able to stand on my own, she never left me. Even when I hit the ground, she never stopped asking God to save me. Unfortunately, I'd forgotten about God.

The Fall

When I was in a bad situation, Kelly didn't hesitate to take me in a few times. I could tell by the look on her face that she just wanted me to get better. She didn't want to see her little brother hiding out, struggling to survive, and addicted. I was in so much trouble that at one of my hearings, the judge told me, "I suggest you leave this county and never come back. I won't be surprised if you end up with a bullet in your head one day." Each time I bought drugs I constantly put my life at risk.

As long as I refused to change, neither would the situation with Branson. I had to be careful because I couldn't afford to cross the line and make enemies. This was the life I'd chosen and I believed that the people in it were my family. They couldn't hurt me because I was already hurting and self-medicating was a way to keep the wounds closed. I thought I handled that when I died long ago on the bridge.

Eleven
The Price of a Life

There was a period when money wasn't a problem. But things changed as my habit progressed and sense of responsibility dissipated. Every once in a while I couldn't pay my debt. I'd take what money I had, buy drugs to sell, used more than I sold, and avoided the dealer until I corrected the situation. That's a common mistake of an addict, but I still managed to handle my business. Owing money wasn't a situation I expected to find myself in, but as long as my body was being given what it craved, I didn't care about the consequences, which was an anticipated problem. I sold everything I had and kept going back with whatever I could get my hands on to sell or trade for more drugs. It's an easy way for girls to end up on the street prostituting to sustain their habit.

The Fall

Regardless of the debt I incurred, sooner or later, I didn't have a choice but to return to the dealer and pay it. Besides, there were only two options in the matter. Necessary resources would cut me off or I'd end up dead because they don't have a pardon for addicts. Whatever the problem or excuse was, they've heard it before. If drug dealers had a conscious, they wouldn't have a productive business or they'd be dead. Whether or not they cared to admit it, the majority of them had someone to answer to in regards to financial obligations. Those were the people the cops were trying to stop, why the DEA was looming about, and the Fed's wouldn't go away. Drugs were being made and they couldn't prevent its filthy evolution fast enough to save lives or their city. Once the borders to California were patrolled, dealers found a more resourceful way to make money. Clandestine labs could be established practically anywhere because the supplies were already available.

My buddies and I used to go into drugstores, slip in the back, and steal boxes of pills to sell to the dealers. They'd cook it down and make meth. We'd hit all of the stores as often as we could until they caught on.

Cain was one of the bigger dealers running the scene. When I needed something I had other connections that I could go to, but he was easily accessible. He'd let me buy on consignment because he knew I'd be back with his cash as soon as I sold the product or he'd send one of his henchmen to find me.

I began to do more business with Cain, but there was an incident where I was negligent in repaying him on time. I owed Cain thirty dollars, but I didn't have it because I used it to get through the day. You don't take the chance of running into a guy like that, or any of his crew, when you're in debt. Knowing this, I stayed away thinking I could evade him for a few days until I had the money. It made me reflect upon the way I'd dodge my father if I knew he'd be upset for any reason, warranted or not.

Late one evening, I was home flipping through the channels trying to find something on television. I ran across a show I used to watch with my siblings and it brought back good memories from my childhood. After our parents had gone to sleep, I'd climb out of bed and knock on the wall adjacent to Kelly's room, alerting her it was time for us to sneak downstairs and watch television. Most of the time, Troy was already down there. We'd stay up for hours watching *The Tonight Show Starring Johnny Carson* followed by back-to-back episodes of the *Honeymooners*. We were convinced our parents wouldn't catch us since they worked from six thirty in the morning until five or six in the evening. We kept the laughter to a hushed tone and made a fun routine out of it. These were some of my best memories with my brother and sister because they didn't go a night without me.

I wasn't in the mood to do anything other than sprawl out on the sofa wearing a pair of shorts and socks while watching an old episode of the *Honeymooners*. Just as I repositioned the pillow beneath my head and took a sip of Jack, someone started pounding on the door. I didn't want to be bothered so I ignored it. Anyone stopping over that late was nothing more than a purchase. I needed the money but I was too high to care. Seconds later, the pounding increased, rattling my door like someone was trying to knock it down. I frowned as my eyes veered in the direction of the noise and then a familiar voice called out.

"Trick Bag! I know you're in there! Open up man!" I didn't respond so he started giving a long dissertation of my whereabouts. "Trick Bag! Com'on, your car's here! I just saw Rosalyn. She told me you were home. Com'on, open up bro. I need to talk to you!"

"Hold on!" I shouted back, slowly making my way off the sofa. I was irritated because Rosalyn must have left the gate unlocked when she left *again*.

I slammed my bottle of Jack on the coffee table, went over to the door and placed my eye against the peephole. I saw a skinny little guy in a wrinkled, red shirt, about five-foot-eight, rocking back and forth. I waited until he turned around. It was my buddy Jeremy wearing a wolfish expression. His nervous demeanor alluded to something being wrong so I quickly unlocked the deadbolt to let him in.

"What's up, man?"

"You always said, 'when someone wins, someone has to lose' and I didn't want it to be *me* this time," he said pointing at himself.

"What the hell are you talkin' about?"

Before Jeremy could say anything further he was shoved aside like a little kid. Standing in my doorway was scary ass Cain. He was six-foot-six with a black Mohawk and deep scar on his cleft chin extending halfway down his neck. He released a gravely smirk as he stomped into my living room gripping a three-foot metal pole resembling a tire iron with his large hands.

"You owe me money, bitch!"

The Price of a Life

I threw my hands up so he could see I didn't have a weapon and said, "Whoa, calm down. I know–and I'll get it to you."

There was nothing else spoken, Cain took the iron pole and cracked me over the left side of my face so viciously; I thought he caved it in. Warm blood poured down my face and onto my chest. Instantly dazed, I was unable to articulate any words of defense. It gave him the chance to strike me again, and he did, clipping the right side of my head. Using my arm to shield my head stopped the blow from being potentially fatal. I couldn't manifest any thought other than *run*. I took off in a staggering sprint out the house, through a side gate, and into the street where I flagged down a cop car heading in my direction. By the time Cain and Jeremy reached me, I was leaning in the window of the car telling them that I'd just been attacked. By whom, I wasn't dumb enough to say. I told them I didn't recognize the guys. It was like playing tag and the cop car was home base so they couldn't get me. Cain and Jeremy fell back and disappeared in the opposite direction although his return was guaranteed. He'd come after me and what was left of my life would end over *thirty drug dollars*. That's the price of a life on the streets!

Hours later, I called my buddy Hank to find out if Cain was still looking for me. Hank got along with everyone and was able to find out just about anything. He wouldn't lie to me. When he said it was safe I went back home and locked the gate behind me for peace of mind. I didn't feel like dying *that way* and I had to get rid of the pain. My arm and entire left side of my face were swollen, bloody and bruised. I couldn't see anything out of my left eye. Staggering into the bathroom, I cleaned off the blood then returned to the sofa and laid down. I reached for the bottle of Jack and took a long swig. I thought about my snake, Lusi and decided I wasn't willing to give up and die. I had to fight.

I didn't have another alternative, which is why I went to my father's office the next day and asked him for money so I could repay Cain before he killed me. Dad seemed more than distraught with my bruised face, scraggly clothing and sickly appearance, but he reached in his pocket and gave me the money. I don't think he ever imagined me that way and looking into his eyes, it hurt him deeply. Anytime I was in a place where I'd hit rock bottom, my father was there for me. I believe it was due to the guilt he carried because of the way he treated me as a child. Still latent with my own animosity, I would go to Dad because I wasn't ready to change. It was like I was saying, "Look how fucked up I am." He'd take me to lunch, give me some money and then I'd go on my way. I went to Dad because I needed him while I was at my worst, which ran for the same duration of time that he abused me. He never stepped up and apologized. Instead, he tried to give me what I asked for.

The next morning, I called Hank and asked him to stop over so I could give him the money to repay Cain. He went to see him and I waited to find out what more Cain expected. A few hours later, Hank returned and told me he'd spoken with Cain. Since he recouped his thirty dollars, he agreed to let it go. He told me Cain's reputation in the streets had significant merit. "It's not somethin' to fuck with because next time, he said, he'd kill your ass." Hell, we were already dead out there. He'd just make it permanent. Cain only came after me because of the principle, not the amount. When Cain took the money and let me go, I became aware that God was looking out for me.

Looking at my life for what it was escaped my view. I was still taking from life and giving little in return. I'd lost faith in God, which was the biggest mistake I'd ever made because hell was deceptively engulfing me in its inferno.

Part of me wanted the normalcy of a relationship to help calm my cravings for death. I believed Rosalyn was that person, but then too much time passed with us in a state of nothingness. She was incredibly sexy and loyal but that wasn't enough anymore. I needed to be with someone that wasn't a reflection of me. I hoped that if I ever had the chance to meet the right person, it would erase the pain in my past and I could start over. In a subtle way, it seemed like I was being prepared for something, although I didn't know what. Until I did right by the life God gifted me with, I was destined to face one trial after another but I didn't know how to stop it.

When I was left alone with my addiction, I didn't think anything good was possible because I was slowly killing myself, just like Kaleigh. I didn't want anyone to ever take the fall or let go of God's hand the way I had done. I could feel the weight of death upon me and I was finally receptive to God's plan.

The Fall

Twelve
Life

It was two thirty that afternoon and I was about to call Mom when my black pager went off. I wanted to ignore it, but I couldn't. I shoved the last bite of my burrito into my mouth and picked up the phone to call Branson instead. It rang once and he answered like *he* was in a hurry. I could hear him exhaling or more like blowing smoke.

"My sergeant handed me a file on a case we've been workin' for a while. Finally we're close. I need information. I'm givin' *you* two hours to get it and I'm warning you Myers–"

"No *hello*, Detective?"

"Cut the shit."

"Alright then. What do you want?"

"I need an address for a guy by the name of Marco Grimaldi and I wanna know where he'll be tonight."

I heard him take a long drag of his cigarette followed by another drawn-out exhale.

"How do I get an address for someone I don't know?"

"Ask."

"If I haven't heard of him already, it's not recommended to go askin' around out of the blue like that."

"I don't give a damn how you get the information, Myers, but I want it. Two hours. That's it. When you get that address, find out what kind of inventory he has."

"Inventory?"

"That's what I said."

"How do you suggest I do that?"

"I don't know. Pull a few tricks out of your bag and make shit happen."

"You don't get how these people work. Grimaldi sounds like part of the cartel and I don't want anything to do with them."

He laughed, "You're kiddin' me, right? Those guys are your brothers. You have their drugs flowin' through your veins. Now stop with the excuses and find Grimaldi."

"Why is this guy so important? Cant you just–"

"Do you remember, Carp? You know him as–"

"Of course I remember him."

"There's more at stake here than you know. Carp was a good detective and his father–was my partner. He was loyal to you for as long as I can remember. Why? I don't have a clue. What I do know is that he had hope you'd get your life together. That's why he asked me to do everything in my power to keep your sorry ass out of prison. He didn't want you stuck in the system. The only way to do that was by makin' you my informant, but you can't even do that right."

"I–I didn't know."

"But now that you do–if you gave a damn about Carp, you'll get me what I need."

"Why didn't you tell me this before?" There was no reply. "Branson!"

After spitting out his orders he hung up. I grabbed my ball cap and headed for the front door.

"Hold on. It's New Year's Eve."

I turned around to find Rosalyn standing there wearing a soft teal sweater and jeans. Evidently she overheard my conversation. Her expression hadn't changed from the same look of disapproval I'd grown accustomed to.

"You're not going to spend the night running around like an errand boy for that detective. What's that about anyways?"

"I don't have a choice. Look, I need to go and I should be back in a few hours."

"Here you go again with the–'I don't have a choice'. You *do* have a choice," she said shaking her head. "Todd, this has to end. That cop, Branford–"

"Branson."

"His name's irrelevant. The problem is that he controls your every move. You'll be dead if you keep this up. For once, just look at your life."

"I know and I will. But right now, I'm doin' everything I can to stay above ground. As for ending this, I'll figure that out. I will."

"When, Todd?"

"I'm workin' on it. Why do you think I'm runnin' and jumpin' every time I'm paged? I have to be out there until I-"

"Once again, more excuses. I don't want this anymore, for either of us."

"Okay, well let's see if you feel that way when I get back. Better yet, you can leave anytime you want. I don't need this shit right now."

"Really, Todd? This isn't who you are and it's not who I am either," she confessed.

"You weren't sayin' that shit last night when you were beggin' for me to-"

"This isn't about sex! It's about you."

"Today it's about me, huh? Funny how you don't seem to care when we're in bed or when I'm givin' you what you want."

"Todd! Please, listen. This isn't what *I* want," she said putting her hand up against her breast as though she was hurting. Tears formed in her misty eyes before rolling down her cheeks.

Sadly, there was nothing she could say to make me stay. With both hands, she smoothed her hair off of her face and then reached inside of her purse sitting on the countertop. She pulled out three large hairpins and began twisting her hair into a neat bun. When she finished, she placed her hands on her hips and studied the details of my face.

"Don't cry, baby. Listen, it's not as bad as it seems. I'm used to it. I'm doin' the best I can just like you are."

I took three steps towards her but she quickly put her hand up and backed away.

"They can use you as long as you're an addict. They give you money to make buys and they sure as hell don't care if you beg, buy and destroy your life with meth, coke, alcohol or anything else!"

"Rosalyn–maybe Branson's not using me. Maybe he's tryin' to protect me."

"Are you blind? From what?"

"I don't know."

Is this all your life will ever be? Do you hate it so much that you want to die this way?"

My eyes darted towards the door. "I have to go. If I don't–"

"This isn't meant for you. Look at yourself."

"Yeah well, look in the mirror. It's not meant for you either."

When she turned around to begin pacing the living room floor, I slipped out the front door letting it slam behind me.

Traffic was heavy, giving me time to think as I drove over to Hank's. I figured he'd know who Grimaldi was and if he didn't, he'd tell me who could help me find out. Branson was more adamant about getting information on Grimaldi than anyone else. And I didn't need Branson telling me Carp was loyal; I already knew it. Even from his grave, he was still looking out for me. When I knocked on his door, his mother immediately answered. She said Hank was unavailable and quickly shut the door in my face.

I didn't know anyone else that could give me information about the mysterious Grimaldi. If he existed, I wasn't convinced that he was in Pleasanton because I'd know. If he needed to arrest me, perhaps that would be best for everyone since things were already bad. I had a couple dealers after me because I owed them money. As for Rosalyn, she knew what she needed and perhaps it would be better for her if she left.

The Fall

My mind drifted and I couldn't help but think about Mom. For some reason, I kept hearing her words over and over in my head. She kept telling me to *get up*. I needed to call her before the end of the day.

I drove across town so I could climb out my invisible escape hatch back into my imaginary safe place. I went there when I was hurting. Down by the stream is where I spent a great deal of my childhood playing, thinking, crying and then dying. I trampled through the heavy weeds and thought about what I was doing. For the first time, I looked up at the bridge and shook my head contemptuously. *What had I done?* I rested my hands on top of my head and let out an echoing scream.

I allowed my world to be shattered by my anger and I wasn't built to fall like that. I was thirty-two years old and had lost many seasons to obscurity. I had a beautiful family that didn't deserve to watch me suffer in my world with death hovering over me. When I was a child, I thought almost everything about my life was as bad as it could possibly get, but I was wrong. It didn't compare to anything I experienced after the fall.

I dropped down on the grass and sobbed heavily for several minutes. Trying to hide from my childhood, I made one bad decision after another. If my father ever thought he would have contributed to me destroying my life, he never would have hurt me. He didn't know.

"Todd."

It was Mom's serene voice. I turned my head and looked behind me. She was walking towards me.

"Mom?"

She stood directly in front of me and looked down with a peaceful radiance.

"Come on. You've got to *get up*, Todd."

"How did you know I was here? Wait. Where'd you come from?"

I turned and looked up towards the street to see where she parked or if Denny was with her. She was alone and I didn't see her car. I didn't see any car.

"That doesn't matter," she replied. She moved closer to me, bent down, and rubbed her hand soothingly across my back. "What are you doing, Todd? This isn't what life is about. You've got to stop this. I know you're hurting. We've all been hurt by one thing or another, but it's not worth doing this to yourself."

"You saw what he did to me. You were there."

"No, Todd. Your father didn't do *this* to you. Remember, I *was* there. God knows I didn't allow him to do that to me. My childhood had its share of hurt, and so did your father's, but the choices we make belong to us. And yours are what caused this to happen."

"Mom, I don't know how to fight hate."

"You're not fighting hate, Todd, you're fighting God. You're wasting the life God gave you and it wasn't meant for any of this."

"But this is all I know."

"No, Toddy. It's all you've chosen. I love you enough to *let you fall* because it's how you'll learn. The difference is that I won't let you go. If I do, you won't have the rest of your life. You need to acknowledge your lessons and start fighting to change."

"How, Mom? Please tell me."

The Fall

"Let's start right now. It's time for you to *get up* so you can begin. When you get through everything, you'll have an amazing life. You'll see. Trust God."

I wiped the tears from my eyes and when I stood up, Mom was gone. My brain was wrapped in dense fog.

———————

Mom was right; I had to get up. I'd done it before because of her pleading with me and if I made the choice to do it again, it wouldn't be easy, but I could. I stayed by the stream for a few minutes longer reminiscing about the last time Mom implored me to fight.

In the ninth grade, I'd become increasingly lethargic and frail because I'd been sick for a while, but my father thought I was playing for sympathy. The difference was evident in my weight and overall demeanor. The day I was at my worst, Dad tried to make me drink a smoothie because I hadn't been eating. However, my body had surrendered to the virus and stress. I couldn't drink it *because I couldn't breathe!* Dad didn't believe anything was wrong even while I was gasping for air, but Mom knew better. She rushed me to the hospital, whereas my father refused to go. I had a temperature of one hundred and five degrees when we arrived. While the doctor had me prepped for surgery in contemplation of doing a tracheotomy, Mom called my father to let him know what was going on, but he maintained his position that nothing was wrong with me. Mom slammed the phone down and dropped to her knees.

"Save my son and take away my marriage," was all she said.

The doctor had known us for a long time and I detected the sympathy he had for Mom. It bothered me to hear my mother pleading with the doctor, "You have to save my son's life!" When I glanced over, Mom's tears were so heavy it hurt me.

Although I escaped having a tracheotomy, they admitted me to the hospital to be treated for Mononuelicous Epstein-Barr Virus, which attacked my immune system and made me lethargic. Mom stayed by my side. However, the doctor let her know I wasn't showing any improvement. Mom went right back to doing what she did best and continued to pray with complete faith.

When the doctor returned to the room she told him, "As soon as you can, you have to make him well!"

"I can't make him well if he doesn't want to be," he replied, glancing over at me before returning his attention to Mom. "And right now, he doesn't care to live."

His words did something to Mom because she refused to accept them. With strength in her voice, she reached for my hand and told me, "Toddy, whatever you want–I'll get it! But you have to fight!"

I'd never seen my mother desperate until then and I didn't want to see her in that kind of pain.

With a weak smile I said, "I want a walkman, public school, and Dad out of the house."

"Whatever you want!"

The Fall

It was getting late and I had a strange sense of receptiveness infiltrating my consciousness. Pretty soon every club would be packed and the parties would be in full swing. I had a lot weighing heavily on my soul and needed to determine where I should begin. I decided to stop at the corner store, pick up some chew, and then call Branson because the time frame he'd given me had passed. He paged me but I didn't hear it go off at the time because I was talking with Mom. I parked out front and when I headed towards the door, I saw Kaleigh coming out.

"How's it goin'? You look–"

"Clean?"

"That too, but I was gonna say *better* since the last time I saw you."

Her lips curved up releasing a broad smile and she replied, "Yeah, well, I'm trying."

"That's what counts. You know, I was thinkin' that maybe it's time for me to try too."

"This isn't what we're supposed to be doing with our pain, Todd. Although I was out of it when I saw you last, you said something that resonated with me. You whispered, *'Ross wouldn't want you suffering this way.'*"

"No. He wouldn't. It would–"

"I know," she said rubbing my arm. "But he wouldn't want this for you either. You were family to Ross and you're the one that encouraged him to follow his passion and become a cop in the first place. He never forgot how you beat the crap out of Big Barry for him and that–that meant the world to him. It made him want to protect people the same way you did him." I began choking up and briefly turned away to hide my watering eyes. She continued, "I'm heading back to school to work on my master's in a couple days. I've been on break long enough," she said letting out a sweet laugh.

"You were a psych major, right?"

She nodded. "I want to help people handle their problems better so they don't end up like me. I've been clean for three years now," she said showing me the sobriety bracelet.

"I'm–I'm really proud of you," I said smiling at her. I thought that's what Ross would have said.

"You can do this too you know. I mean–it's not easy. But, what the hell, it's worth trying 'til we get it right."

On the opposite side of the street, I noticed an unfamiliar car with slightly tinted windows pull alongside the curb. A few minutes passed but no one got out.

"Those guys in the black Mercedes over there, are they waitin' for you?"

She bent down to glance at them, but they turned away.

"I don't think so, but it's hard to tell."

"Fuck that!"

"Let it go," she said grabbing hold of my arm. "You can't be suspicious of everyone. I'm really trying to get my life back and not shut down the way I did before. I can't be afraid anymore. That's what was killing me. Fear. I'm working towards getting past what happened and I can. I can do this."

Kaleigh was beautiful, especially when her jade eyes smiled at me. I could smell the rose and violet scent of her perfume.

"Hold on a sec while I run in the store. I'll give you a ride. Where you headed?"

The Fall

"I'm going to say goodbye to a friend off Bernal Ave. My car is right around the corner."

"I'll walk you to it."

"I'm fine. Really."

"I don't like the way—"

"I can't spend my life being paranoid. I did that already and it wasn't helping. And look at you. You probably think everyone's a threat. But when you get your life together, you won't have anything to worry about. Right?"

I nodded in agreement.

Kaleigh gave me a really long hug and began walking away. Suddenly, she turned around, blew me a kiss off of her pink lips and waved as she turned the corner. Seeing her did something for me and I was extremely happy for her. Thinking about Ross hit me where I needed it most. I made a quick run in the store. When I came out, the Mercedes was gone. She was probably right about me being paranoid so I shook it off, got in my car and headed home.

When I walked through the door, the warm smell of amber and vanilla lingered in the air, but the candle didn't mask the underlying odor. Rosalyn was sitting on the sofa with the television on, but she wasn't watching it. I could tell she'd been waiting for me. She was upset because it was New Year's Eve and she hadn't heard from me since I left hours earlier. I told her I was down by the stream thinking, hurting, and just trying to figure things out. The conversation was fine until I brought up Mom. Before I could tell her how positive it was, Rosalyn got up, walked into the kitchen, and picked up the phone to call someone. Just before dialing, she paused as if she knew something that I didn't.

"Your Mom called here looking for you twenty minutes ago, Todd. She said she hasn't heard from you in a few days."

"What the hell are you talkin' about? I was by the stream and she found me there."

"Look, I know you call her every two days regardless of what's going on, but you didn't call her today and you definitely didn't see her. How can you stand there and lie to me about your mother?"

"I was with her."

The conversation escalated into an argument and everything faded to black.

The Fall

Thirteen
The Awakening

The negative thoughts that randomly infiltrated my mind made it necessary for me to change focus and pray or read the Bible to strengthen my challenged spirit. I was learning what I needed because God had spiritually awakened me. It took thirty-two years for me to realize the way I was dying was not my destiny.

I was sitting in the cell crying violently. It was as though any negative data that was programmed inside of me was being removed. I was broken, desperate, and needed for all of it to be gone. It was like going into a computer and deleting a virus that was corrupting all of the good files. The only thing that made sense was for me to continue praying for God to heal my soul. I needed to be forgiven for anyone that I'd hurt and I couldn't complete the process if I didn't forgive anyone that hurt me.

I never cried so long or hard in all my life. When I wasn't sleeping, eating or reading the Bible, I cried. It went on for twenty-five to thirty hours straight. Finally, the revelation of how broken I was hit me, which allowed me to realize that I was blessed by being so broken.

I learned that I made the mistake of trying to hold onto everything. When I arrived at a point of desperation, that's when I came to understand that the only one who could remove it all and set me free was God. Everything keeping me together was nothing more than toxic glue. I didn't want any of my painful history because I was tired of carrying it. It was time for me to let go.

My behavior was so irrational that I was placed on suicide watch. They didn't understand what was taking place because it was bigger than what they could identify with. A guard frequently entered the cell and ordered me to wake up just to make sure I was alive. Everything I was feeling and experiencing was happening for the first time and my heart never felt that way before. The positivity flowing through it caused me to think about others even more than I had. The empathy and compassion I felt brought about something profoundly inspirational.

For the past several years, I made everything about me. My world was comprised of every measure of harm and hurt that I experienced throughout my life. It captured my earliest recollections of hate, rage, abuse, and pain that led me to the bridge. The fall allowed me to transcend as Trick Bag in a life where expectations didn't exist. My self-destructive behavior and negative thoughts are what locked me behind bars. And that was precisely where I needed to be until it was time for me to wake up.

The next morning, I opened my eyes and it seemed as if something had changed with my vision. I noticed all of the colors in the cell and even the dullest of them were brighter. My appreciation for life was at a level that I'd never experienced or knew was possible to achieve. It all came from that moment—*when I woke up spiritually.*

I dropped to my knees again and prayed for God to get me out of the hole. I couldn't take being alone with my thoughts.

Twenty minutes later, a voice over the intercom instructed me to get my things together. I rolled up my mattress and pillow, shoved my belongings inside of it and waited. Within ten minutes, a guard entered my cell and said, "Let's go." He moved me into protective custody and the first thing I noticed was the television. I could play dominoes and talk to people instead of being alone in a white room. I felt like I was pulled out of a speeding car right before it crashed. I didn't think I was worthy of praying for anything when I had given God nothing, but I did, and God was revealing His presence. I believe God was telling me, *I see your potential and I want you to prove to me that you want this. I am going to answer your last prayer.*

I was in the midst of understanding my journey and it didn't matter what my sentence was going to be. I couldn't wait to call my mom and tell her what was transpiring. When the guard took me to make my call I erupted with an unbridled passion.

"Mom! I had the most amazing experience over the past two or three days. I cried hysterically because I've gone through somethin' I can't describe.

The Fall

I had a physical, spiritual and emotional change. Mom, I felt this white light, like a flowing river, go through my heart and out of my body. I cried tears of joy because I was reconnected to my spirit–to my soul! It was like I woke up this morning and started feeling a way that I can't really explain. Mom, I'm gonna be fine. Oh my God, I'm gonna be okay!"

"When are you going to be sentenced?"

"Soon, but it doesn't matter. I get it! I get it now! There's nothing that's gonna detour me from how I feel right now. I fucking get it! I'm fine."

"Amazing."

"I gotta go. Bye!" I hung up the phone.

This was like the best drugs I'd ever done in my life and I was stone cold clean and sober. I was on fire! You could have put me on stage next to Michael Jackson and I would have thrown down!

———

Accepting that I had to be taught how to adjust socially, mentally and physically without substances should have been difficult to face, but not that time. I believed God removed that hunger because I didn't think about it or feel it. The closer I went to God, the more He filled me with light until there was nothing dark inside of me.

Being locked up made sobriety possible, but more importantly, it removed everything that kept me from God. The truth of the situation is that an addiction to meth is like having a chronic disease that doesn't have a cure. This is where my faith and relationship with God had to prevail or nothing else would work. I closed my eyes and thought about the first time that *I* wanted to build a relationship with God.

———————

By seventh grade, my Attention Deficit Disorder was through the roof. Every morning I'd go to Express Liquors and buy cases of Now and Later's, Starburst, and Red Devil Jawbreakers. I bought them for ten cents each and then sold them from thirty to fifty cents a pack and tripled my money. With that kind of stash, I was constantly shoving candy in my mouth and I'm sure it didn't help my ADD but it tasted good. Stealing hall passes, selling candy and cutting class got me expelled from Pleasanton Middle School or PMS as it was called, so Mom enrolled me into Valley Christian Center, which was a private school. I ended the seventh grade by failing everything because I refused to try or even care. I spent more time making other kids laugh, which in return, made me happy.

One afternoon, a couple of classmates and I were shooting spitballs at one another when the teacher turned around and slammed her book shut. She caught me with the straw in my mouth and sent the three of us to the office. The principal came out into the waiting area, holding a paddle with a taped up handle, as if we'd made her day. After having a nice time swinging that thing back and fourth against our butts, she made sure we had an extra layer of trouble by notifying our parents. As for the consequences, I didn't think about them until afterwards.

The Fall

I arrived home and found my mother slouched over on the sofa with her face in a pillow. I shut the door and she lifted her head to see who it was. Her face was wet, and her eyes were bloodshot red with traces of black mascara below them. Her whimpers continued to escape while she shook her head in disappointment. She knew.

My mother was more upset with my ongoing dismissive behavior than I'd ever seen her. After years of my escalating behavioral issues, she let it out and I was on the receiving end of Mom's wrath for the first time.

The way I functioned was predicated on how Mom felt about me. Disappointing her in any way hurt me more than she ever knew. I didn't understand what I was doing to her until that specific day. After that, I decided to begin again. I planned to work harder to avoid conflict or creating any problems for her because the situation with my father was already bad.

The kids I went to school with believed in God and the Holy Spirit. In order for me to get the most out of my environment, I made a conscious effort to open up and pray. Really pray.

Within a couple months of starting eighth grade, I elevated my grade point average to a 3.8 and became the president of my class. Nothing mattered to me other than pleasing my mother, but it drained me. I made a conscious effort to be good because I wanted her to be able to function without the stress I was adding to her life. I hated the turmoil my father created and at that point, I was contributing to it.

The problems with Dad persisted without fail. Regardless, for nearly fifteen months, I maintained an intense academic regimen. After several weeks, I couldn't keep up with that pace and the only thing I could manage to do was sleep.

It was the first time I really worked towards a relationship with God that didn't involve my mother. And through proper communication, my teacher taught me why a relationship with God was crucial and how to obtain it. She said it was a lifelong commitment. Yes, I prayed sometimes at dinner, but I never really understood the concept of God.

One of my teachers, Mr. Sykes, was the owner of the place that my BMX bikes were purchased. He taught me that the concept of having an actual relationship with God was different than just praying. It gave me a deeper and much stronger understanding of what life was about on an entirely different level. I understood it and my life was becoming better because of it. I was doing well in school although I was still getting beaten at home. I was more focused on hiding how I felt inside.

The Fall

Fourteen
Begin Again

My arrest on January 1, 2001 brought about an opportunity for me to have a new beginning, even if it was behind bars.

My attorney, Mark Liston, met me again to prepare my defense for my upcoming court date. Over the past few weeks, he learned more about me. I was determined to turn my life around so I didn't offer him any excuses or lies.

I told him the truth about everything. I explained why I became a confidential informant and how Branson gave me money to make purchases so I could go deeper in the game. The people he wanted me to intertwine with were hardened criminals that wouldn't think twice about killing me. Although I was transparent about being an informant, it didn't mean everyone was going to accept it or trust me. I had guns pointed at my head and received death threats because of what the cops were trying to make me do. And they wondered *why* I deflected them elsewhere. Though it may not have been what they wanted, I gave them enough to go on. I wasn't going to be a rat and send them after my friends, whom I considered family when I was out there doing the same thing. I never had the desire to go deeper; that was their goal. I was tired of being used because it only made it difficult for me to change. If I didn't pull it together, when I got out, Branson or some other detective would return and I'd end up in the same situation.

I didn't withhold anything that happened on New Year's Eve. I wasn't going to buy any drugs and I didn't want to be tempted. That's why I went home. I wanted to spend the evening with Rosalyn because I didn't feel good about the way we left things earlier that day.

I told him about seeing my mother, our conversation, and how her words stayed on my heart. When I got home, Rosalyn and I had a heated conversation. I didn't remember much else because I crashed after being up for nearly five days straight. I woke up, showered, and that's when Branson apprehended me. At the time, I didn't know why.

"Okay. I have another question for you." He took a few photos out of a yellow envelope and slid them in front of me. "Do you know this person?"

"Yeah. That's Kaleigh Carpenter. Why?"

"She was found dead last night. Raped with a needle hanging out of her arm in an alley."

I let out a reverberating cry, "Nooooo! No! No!" Shielding my face with both hands, I threw my head back to somehow keep the tears in but I was

138

unsuccessful. I had flashbacks of every beautiful memory of Kaleigh ending with the kiss she blew before turning the corner. I could tell something wasn't right but I let her go. I started choking and wheezing like I was suffocating on his words. Mark quickly opened a bottle of water and handed it to me.

"Who did this? Who in the hell did this to Kaleigh?"

"We were hoping you could tell us?"

"What? How would I know?" I asked defensively.

"We believe it's the same guy Branson's been looking for. A witness placed him and another guy in the alley with Kaleigh around the time of her death–"

"Murder! And she wasn't using. I saw her last night and she was headin' back to school in a few days."

"Hold on. We believe you. Carp–I'm sorry, I mean Ross Carpenter–"

"What about Ross?"

"His death wasn't an accident. That's what the cops wanted the public to think while they were investigating the case. One of Grimaldi's henchmen killed him because Ross was starting to dig too deep. When Kaleigh returned for the funeral, she went to his place to pack up some of her brother's things. She happened to be there when Grimaldi and his guy broke in to get whatever evidence they believed Ross might have had. After brutally raping and beating Kaleigh, they left her for dead. Grimaldi disappeared for a while and the trail went cold. They assumed he returned to Mexico without knowing that she survived."

"That's why she took the fall," I mumbled.

"Sorry, what was that?"

"I was just thinkin' out loud."

The Fall

Mark continued, "Then, one day, Branson saw her again. She asked for his help and he placed her in rehab outside of Pleasanton. Apparently, the day you saw her, she was here to say goodbye."

"To who?"

"Branson. He said Kaleigh was supposed to call him when she was in town so he could make sure he was at the station. He didn't want to miss seeing her. He was proud of her accomplishments."

"She called–"

"And what?"

"And told him she'd be there shortly, but she never made it." He reached in the envelope and pulled out another photo. "The camera outside the building caught this," he said pointing at the tattoo. "But, it didn't capture his face." It was a picture of a guy with a black sleeveless t-shirt displaying a Mexican Horned Pit Viper wrapped up his arm. *This is who Branson's looking for. If you know Grimaldi's whereabouts–"

"Shit! That's not Grimaldi! That son-of-a-bitch is the Reaper! She told me he had a big snake with horns on his arm! I didn't get it until now."

On February 9, 2001, Mark Liston was reviewing his notes. Dressed in a smart blue suit, heavily starched white shirt, and a blue and white striped tie, Mark appeared new to the profession. His blue eyes smiled with an optimistic glimmer. I took a deep breath while I sat at the table in handcuffs waiting for

140

the judge. He sat his coffee on the table, reached inside his briefcase and pulled out another manila file with a white label that had my name on it. Apprehensively, I looked over my shoulder to see if Rosalyn, Mom, Denny, Dad, Kelly or Troy had come to my sentencing. No one was there. I didn't expect them to show and I wasn't sure when I'd see them again. I couldn't imagine that any of them would want to see me in handcuffs and leg irons being taken away for several years.

Mark patted me on my back and asked, "Are you ready?"

I shrugged and replied, "I don't have a choice."

Right before the judge entered the courtroom, Mark looked across at Branson and gave a slight nod. Branson returned one. Then he turned to me and said, "Well, you're lucky Detective Branson didn't go after you with all of the initial charges he had. The information you gave him regarding Grimaldi gave them what they needed. He's been charged with the murders of both Ross and Kaleigh Carpenter. With the arsenal of weapons, drugs, underage sex ring, and money laundering, he's looking at life. You did a good thing in making sure their killer didn't go free." He patted me on the back but all I could do was try to hold it in at the thought of both Ross and Kaleigh. He cleared his throat and continued. "At any rate, you're going to do time since you've violated the terms of your probation. We'll see if the judge has any leniency after talking with Branson. You don't want the max because it'll put you in San Quentin with Grimaldi. You're looking at five to seven years but I'm trying to get a suspended sentence with rehab to help you get your life together. I'm confident Branson wants that too."

The Fall

I took a deep breath, dropped my head, and prayed.

Rehab

During my time in jail, I stayed focused on healing and the primary way to do it was by re-establishing my relationship with God. I craved being in the chapel and it always had a fresh smell, like it was recently built. Out of one hundred and fifty men, there were usually only two or three guys in the chapel when I was there. Time forced the initial stages of my recovery, which lasted for two months. I went through withdrawal and when that stage ended, I felt better than I had in a long while.

When depression resurfaced, it attempted to hit me harder than expected and I began dwelling on the difficulties of my childhood. Immediately, I felt unplugged again. My heart didn't feel like it was there and blood started filling up in my chest. I was scared, but I kept praying for God to take it all away. When I saw the physician, I told him I needed a mood stabilizer to keep me from feeling anxiety and something to help me sleep. He gave me Wellbutrin and Trazodone since I'd been on them before.

After two months in jail, I was released to serve the balance of my bullet, or year, in the drug rehabilitation center, Diablo Valley Ranch. At that point, my sole focus was sustaining sobriety and creating a better life. I had to prepare for the challenges awaiting me so I could overcome them rather than hide.

At nineteen, I got into trouble but eluded jail with a suspended five-year sentence as an alternative. Even with that, nothing changed. I went right back to what I knew because I didn't acknowledge my relationship with God. Somehow, *this time*, I didn't believe anything about the situation was a coincidence or luck. God knew my heart and I knew what God wanted me to do. The caveat was that I had to go to rehab and finish the program or I would end up back in jail to conclude the rest of my sentence.

Having my freedom created the opportunity for me to get high at any given point because rehab didn't have a wire fence and guards with guns. God knew what I needed and understood the necessity of my journey. When I was in the hole, God granted me the strength and spiritual awakening I desired. He knew at that particular time in my life, I was ready and willing.

I felt healthier, but I had a lot of work ahead of me because I refused to relapse. I spent a lot of time studying the Bible and trying to find a way to address my demons. Rehab would help me grow stronger if I committed to making a significant transformation.

What I finally realized was that those changes would contribute to helping me shape my life.

When the ranch had family day, I couldn't wait to see Mom and Kelly. Rosalyn had understandably moved on with her life but I continued to pray for her to find what I had. I understood the fight ahead of me but after seeing them, I was more determined to make it work. *I'd rather fail trying to do something than doing nothing.* I was being taught to stay away from the environment I played in and the people I hung out with. It was possible for anything familiar to cause a setback. I had a list of things that I was warned not to do. For some strange reason, deep in my heart, I believed God had already healed me in jail. In fact, I was positive He had.

Going through withdrawals in jail was the beginning of removing toxic chemicals from my body. However, the remnants of them and whatever physical damage I did would be there for a long time, if not permanently. Getting the hate and anger out was equally important to my recovery so when I had counseling sessions, I let it go.

The rehab facility was filled with men just like me. Some of them were fresh from jail while others were trying to avoid it. There were those that had an intervention and a handful that came on their own. I remembered when Mom took me to rehab after putting together my first intervention. It didn't work because I didn't want it to.

My family had no other recourse but to go on with their lives. I suspected there came a point when they, too, faced reality and accepted that I would most likely die from an overdose or living recklessly. It was the plan I'd set in motion.

The Fall

Rehab offered me something different and this time, I accepted it. I wasn't alone; there were dozens of men living there with me. They too, made the choice to hide their pain, deficiencies, or history by abusing a substance rather than addressing their problems. I had to be willing to acknowledge the truth and rehab was going to make me confront my demons. Until then, I didn't want to take responsibility and lying was the way to avoid it.

It was imperative to stay away from the wrong people and grow closer to God regardless of the distractions. My diligence in studying the Bible was what gave me the strength to do that. I began with Psalms and was captivated with what I was reading so I continued with Proverbs and just kept going. The words in the Bible meant more to me than food and water. I believed that if I had understanding, it would put me in a place that would make my aura stronger and more peaceful. Praying for understanding eliminated the threat of animosity towards others. God had a plan for me and He wanted me to follow Him.

People have different stages in their lives where pain is more prevalent than others. Even though I always thought those years were during my childhood, I was wrong. My life was in the middle of a demolition from 1996 to 2000 making those years the most disturbing. I couldn't escape until the following year.

The power of rehab is largely underestimated. It won't work until you accept that something is going to win the fight for your soul; it will be life or death. I knew my family loved me and more than anything, they wanted me to get my life together. I had a chance to recover if I wanted it bad enough, and I took it.

Rehab was at a self-running ranch because it was a non-profit, ninety-day program. There were seventy men on the ranch and six counselors. Each house held fourteen men and every one of us were afraid to go back on the streets. To keep that from happening, I went to thirteen meetings and five Bible studies each week. On Friday's we had counseling sessions and every house was checked to make sure they were spotless because *cleanliness is next to godliness*. They were teaching us the necessary skills to begin functioning properly again, as well as, establishing healthy routines.

I recalled the chores my father had me do around the house. Doing them brought back the sense of pride I had when Dad paid me. However, I was disappointed when he was upset and would nit-pick over little things. In actuality, whether or not it was intentional, he was teaching me to have higher standards. Once you learn how to do something the right way, it won't escape you. The ranch was teaching us to have higher standards for ourselves and cleanliness was a must.

I was doing well at the ranch because the counselors wouldn't allow my demons to hide there. I continued to take my walks up to the little brown chapel where I'd sit in silence, reflect, and pray. I was literally at my best when I was there, in the presence of God.

The chapel had four pews on both the left and right side, a podium in the middle, and a window behind it. There was a perfect view to the isolated upthrust peak of Mt. Diablo that appeared to be a double pyramid. I loved the peace and comfort from being in the chapel because it felt cleansing and cathartic. I knew where to go when I needed God and how to reach Him but I never felt worthy. When I was doing what was right, I felt closer to God and better about praying. God had given me time to grieve, hurt, complain, and get it all out. Now it was time to stop. I needed to get to that place of peace that Mom found.

What lifted my spirit was the framed picture with the Serenity Prayer hanging on the wall. It brought comfort to my soul each time I read it because I realized that I needed the courage to *change the things I can change*. I was inspired by its truth. Submitting to praying with absolute faith would remove all traces of doubt. It was time for me to accept my blessings rather than experience condemnation.

The smallest acts have a way of evoking a sense of pride in us when we least expect it. But after relinquishing my pride and living without any facet of it for the duration of that journey, it was a blessing when it returned. Pride is a good thing, but when it morphs into arrogance it becomes dangerous.

The facility I was in made it a point to acknowledge our accomplishments. They recognized improvement, which was significant to me, especially after not having made any for nearly two decades. I had fallen into a trap of self-pity, victimization, doubt, and mistrust. I didn't evolve. In fact, every step I took caused me to be thrust ten steps back. I was on the wrong path sabotaging my own happiness and until I changed my course, I would continue living in hell.

When they had award night at the Diablo Valley Ranch, Mom and Kelly came. It was evident they were proud of my willingness to fight. I hadn't seen Mom look at me with that kind of respect in years.

Rehab

Sobriety had more of a temporary affect for most of the men in the program because like me, it was easier to go back to old behaviors. I became a ranch foreman to the seventy guys seeking treatment and I watched almost six hundred men go through the program in ten months. Once they were in the system, we had access to track their progress. Sadly, there were only four men that stayed clean and sober. It was disheartening when someone died or returned to what they knew best. It hit me hard to realize the value of the chance I was given.

Some of the men that were there for the first time thought the process would be easy. They had the idea that they could come in, get clean, and go back to their life full of optimism. From my experience, it doesn't work that way. I'd been to five rehabs that were ineffective. Once I left, everything they taught me was left behind too. Rehab ended up being a temporary resting place to detox and let my body try to recover from being a dumping ground of poisons. Rehab isn't a fast process that you can skim through and just expect it to work.

When I was in the tenth grade, Mom and Denny bought me a 1977 black Camaro Z28 and I loved that car. When I drove it to school, I parked close to the doors to make it easier for me to dart out of there in between classes or during physical education. If I was going to be mischievous, it only made sense to have a plan. I'd sneak out of school with three or four of my buddies and most of the time it was Brian,

Steve, Jeff and John that were ready. We'd grab a dozen Winchell's Donuts, do donuts in their parking lot, and then tear out of there leaving a stream of smoke behind us. I thought it was more fun after it rained because the pavement was slick. I found the thrill of speed to be somewhat of an addiction in itself. When we got back to school, we sold the donuts. I was back in my seat for the next class and everything worked out. It was that fast.

My car was fast, dangerous, and like a drug to me. I didn't identify with the power it possessed nor did I consider the threat that drugs held. I just wanted what I wanted. I raced other kids through town from one stop sign to another, which were usually set a quarter mile apart. At the speed I was going, the possibility of hurting someone else through my reckless behavior didn't cross my mind. I was inside of a selfish realm and it was comfortable there. I listened to hard music, smoked weed, and was rebellious just to show everyone what years of being in pain had done.

When I returned from my recollections, I wished it all had been nothing more than a bad dream. The memories I had while sober often told a truth that I needed to see.

Sixteen
The Fall

Reveling in the thought of letting go of my past filled me with so much excitement I couldn't sleep. It was my final week at the Diablo Valley Ranch. They taught me how to live the right way and I wanted to make good use of my time. I would take everything I learned with me and use it daily. Merely thinking about how far I'd made it humbled me. I had a lot to be thankful for.

Already dressed in a pair of jeans and my black and red AC/DC t-shirt, I slipped into my tennis shoes. The sun was just beginning to make its presence known and I wanted to be a part of the audience. It had been a long time since I appreciated the light but nowadays, I had an insatiable longing for it.

When I left the house, I passed a few of the guys, groggily beginning their chores and smiled as I nodded to them. They were lacking passion and energy because the darkness was weighing them down, just as it had once done to me. I took a walk up the winding dirt trail and inhaled the crisp air as if it were new to me. Until now, everything had been toxic, rancid, or reeked of death.

Every step I took felt good because I felt good. My head was clear, vision focused, and I could feel my heart beating strong. Ahead was a small pond loaded with bass that held my attention for countless hours. I smiled when I reached it because it reminded me of a mirror. I used it as a place to reflect on the decisions that brought me to the ranch. The shimmering water was always clear enough to see the truth.

I used to sit on the bench trying to absorb the twelve steps of the program. The other rehab facilities made me well aware of the steps. However, the distinction was that I finally learned how and why I needed to apply them, and then I did so.

Forgiveness had the biggest impact because I had to forgive my father, along with anyone that hurt me. It didn't happen overnight, but it happened. Additionally, it was imperative for me to learn to forgive myself. There were people that I hurt and I believed my mother was on the top of that list. I often thought about the devastation that my pride caused and the consequences of my actions.

I sat facing the pond and thought about the men fighting for their lives in the five houses behind me. I hoped that they would come to understand what rehab was offering them. It wasn't just a working ranch to complete a rehabilitation program. It was a lifesaving, safe haven for anyone that wanted to learn how to live again. DVR facilitated healing but more importantly, you had the choice to give God your full attention. I worked directly with God to fight whatever demons I had and prayed that these men would do the same.

The guys weren't that reserved when it came to sharing their personal situations or struggles. In fact, most of them were grateful to have someone that cared enough to listen. The sad part was that denial and hopelessness ran rampant among those entering the program. The majority of them in each rotation didn't make it.

The facility was strict about upholding their policies, and breaking them meant you didn't care. They weren't going to allow anyone to discourage or influence others that were trying. The counselors dedicated their lives to inspiring anyone that wanted to fight. They shared their struggles as another level of encouragement. They were proof that the program worked. Denying relatability meant you weren't ready for sobriety. The men that bared their souls with passion, prayer, and tears taught us how to beat addiction. They prepared us for a new beginning and from that point, it was up to us. What the counselors offered was more valuable than anyone knew. They addressed the raw, gritty, truth about addiction and taught us how to overcome a lifetime of temptation.

The most reluctant type of personality to change is someone that's there for obligatory reasons. The first five times I went to rehab the counselors told me they could see I wasn't responsive to the program or open to healing. Since I was anxious to leave, the counselors would say, "I see you want to do more research." It was obvious that I was willing to continue gambling with my life.

The Fall

Skinny and one hundred and forty pounds to big burly, three hundred pound men covered in tattoos would sit down with the counselors and let everything pour out. Like me, they were still someone's children. They could no longer handle their pain or disappointing their families so they were there, fighting. Rehab can help facilitate healing if you use a clear mind and body to connect with God.

The clamoring behind me revealed the official start of the day. The creaking of doors opening and slamming shut, with greetings or light conversation, could be heard. Wafting through the morning air was the sweet smell of breakfast. I turned and rotated my body sideways so I could observe them for a few minutes. "Wow! That's what I looked like when I arrived eight months ago." I didn't see myself that way at the time but rehab was what I needed. I wanted every one of them to make it. I prayed that they could be filled with the same faith and determination that I had because I wasn't ever going back to that life. I got up and followed the trail until I reached the little brown chapel. I opened the door and went inside. It was always full of peace, yet I never understood why it remained empty.

I sat in the front pew, closed my eyes, and bowed my head. It was extraordinary just to be alive. My memory swiftly pulled me back to January 1, 2001 when they lowered my head and placed me in the squad car. Everything that happened was meant to come to pass exactly as it had. I may not have survived any other way. While I was in it, I didn't believe I had any other choice but to continue until *that* life claimed *my* life.

A few days before I was arrested, I felt like demons were closing in on me. I couldn't trust anyone in the game because they were either covering for themselves, the cops, or dealers. Before Branson, I had some friends, but not in the end. He made sure of it. Other than Hank, no one was there for me. All doors were closed.

Rebuilding your life takes consistent effort but even then, it won't work without faith stemming from an unyielding relationship with God. Guilt blocked my ability to be receptive and I didn't feel worthy. The breaking point was my mother's words that continued to manifest inside of me *like faith as small as a mustard seed* we once planted together. Now I had the chance to hold on to my relationship with God, just as Mom had done.

Unlike being high or intoxicated, it was essential for me to be present and focused all the time. Most of the work went towards removing excuses. I could have filled dumpsters full of the excuses I'd made over the years. They'd become such a habitual part of my communication that I didn't realize how first nature it was to blame something or someone else for my failures. Refusing to accept responsibility prevented me from addressing the problems and more importantly, fixing them.

Making an investment in rebuilding my life was a vital part of my success and I didn't expect someone else to do it for me. I accepted what I was doing wrong, determined what changes needed to be made, and then did the work with consistency and passion. I focused on changing the things I could. I was realistic in my expectations and diligent in my faith. It was difficult until it became a routine and ultimately transformed into an integral part of me.

Habits can either be good or bad. Since I was clean and sober, I was able to evaluate mine with clarity and without defensive or negative emotions. It helped me understand why I did specific things and what needed to change. While I was developing new habits, I had a lot of old ones that needed to be broken and discarded.

I looked up and stared out of the window towards Mt. Diablo and started shaking my head in disbelief. Tears clouded my vision and the mountain disappeared. Never had I experienced anything so powerful in all of my life as the cleansing I had in the hole. Every account of what happened stayed etched in my mind. I understood every bit of what was happening to me and I prayed that Kaleigh had a chance to have her own spiritual awakening before her death.

I thought about being in my cell, plunging into a hard but peaceful sleep. I remembered waking up as if a faucet automatically turned on and flushed all of the toxins out of my body. They came out in hard, painful tears that stemmed from my cavernous areas where all of my secrets were kept. The wells that had filled over many years were finally emptied. By the time I stopped crying, the darkness had been extracted and my body was replenished with light. The burden that plagued me throughout my life was lifted; it was time to live the right way. I recalled the emotional release that took place when I fell to my knees and prayed. I ended my prayers by thanking God for *everything!* When I finished, it was liberating. I felt lighter and much better as if He removed everything. I had to embrace it. Although I was isolated during my spiritual awakening, I felt God was right there next to me, telling me I was going to be okay. *And I believed Him.*

Mom told me that she got down on her knees and accepted God when she was four years old. She never changed course in darkness or in light. I wanted that faith and obedience more than anything because I was certain everything I needed would come from it. I was willing to do the work.

At the end of rehab, my felony probation officer, Ms. Montez, said she'd never seen anyone turn it around the way that I had. I appreciated her faith in me because she was an amazing woman who really cared about people.

Revealing what I've gone through allows me to help others. Until my spiritual awakening, it was impossible to understand my relationship with God the way I do now. I lived like I was programmed to exist only in pain and finally, it was as if I had a chip taken out and replaced with a better one. It was newer, with the capability to help me analyze situations from a healthy perspective instead of from a negative one. The best part was that it connected me to God's will rather than my own.

Everything started in the hole and I had nothing but fear at that time. When I allowed the words in the Bible to infiltrate my consciousness, instead of having the burden of comprehension, it began to resonate inside of me with ease. It was comparable to reading poetry from over two thousand years ago; it touched my soul and transported my mind to a more peaceful place. I wasn't distracted by anything.

I believed being in the hole was a detriment to my mental state. Yet, it was by design that I was detained in a place gifting me nothing other than what God wanted me to have. It was the place for me to have healing and a spiritual awakening that would prepare me to live. It was there that my heart opened up like a door to a safe passage, which was my destiny. *This time, I took the fall to my knees imagining my mother praying right next to me.*

Seventeen
The Waves

I was strolling along the beach in Carmel thinking about how amazing my life is. Yes, I had a turbulent journey but eventually, I bought and paid for it. I wished I hadn't but there was nothing I could do about the past other than to forgive, ask for forgiveness, and then let it slip away with time—grateful it didn't cost me my life.

Holding onto the past the way I'd done was pure destruction and it would have been for anyone. I wouldn't walk away from my pain so it hitched a ride, embedding itself inside of me like a welcomed companion.

The sun carefully warmed my face and the soft streaks of clouds drifted across the blue sky with the wind as its propellers. Light roars of the ocean commanded my attention and spoke to me as if to remind me of God's power. I stopped walking, turned to face the ocean, and spread out my arms as if I were welcoming its vast body. The fresh smell of saltwater trailed up my nostrils reminding me that I was no longer toxic. Watching the white caps on the waves coming in was simply majestic. It reminded me of my life. Sometimes the waves were rough and attempted to pull me under, but each one offered another opportunity to get up and ride it. I buried my toes in the cool white sand and appreciated being there. *I was finally standing.*

The mistake we make is that we don't take the time to understand our journey or walk away before a negative one consumes us. I could have spent the years creating joyful memories with my family, but instead, I missed them because of my decisions.

Another wave came in and cool water flushed across my feet bringing the thought of Denny along with it. Denny wanted me to have a better life and he would have been proud to see me living this way. It took me a long time to get here but I made it. When I became sober, it was apparent the inspiration he tried to instill in me wasn't wasted.

Denny was certain I would have to endure the challenges I was faced with in order to learn from them. Regardless of how many times he tried to teach me to do the right thing, I think we both silently agreed that the damage was done. I didn't have the fight to beat the addiction back then. It wasn't Denny's fault and there was nothing he could do to prevent it.

Once you know the depth of your damage, you understand that it takes something more powerful than man to save you. My mother was aware of that, which is why she never let me go, but she continued to pray and ask God to save me because no one else could.

Mom and Denny were married when I was a freshman in high school and remained married until he passed away of lung cancer. We buried Denny on November 6, 2007; it was his birthday. It hurt me to think of how much I'd hurt Denny because he tried to be what I needed. However, I discovered what I needed most was God.

It was difficult to watch Mom without Denny because she loved him and he adored her. That was the main reason I loved Denny the way I did. He made Mom smile from her soul until he became ill.

My mother remained the matriarch of our family and I am certain her prayers had the most value. Without them, I would have met death a long time ago. No one could have taken her place and managed to prevail with the grace and strength that she displayed.

While Denny was losing his battle to cancer, so was my grandmother. Mom was extremely close with her mother. I thought the loss of both, Denny and my grandmother, would completely devastate Mom. God appeared to repair everything that was tearing Mom apart and each time, she became stronger and wiser.

Some people have faith that comes in waves depending upon how their life is going. However, I never saw my mother lose her faith, even when she was hurting. She stayed resolute and allowed God to handle each situation accordingly.

With that recollection, I turned and began walking along the beach. Slightly sinking into the cool sand with each footstep, I permitted more memories to return.

The Fall

What I found disappointing was that I couldn't remember many of the things I'd done with my brother and sister while I was suffering through years of addiction. There were things that should have brought incredible laughter, but they were short-lived. Given that I no longer carried the unwanted pain of my childhood, I could see everything more clearly and remembered the things that brought joy to my heart.

I bent down, picked up a broken shell, and held it for a moment. I tossed it into the ocean the way I used to do the newspapers when I had my paper route. I chuckled when I thought of the time I got up early, rode my bike throughout the neighborhood, and delivered them. When I returned home and opened the paper I'd been tossing on everyone's porch, my eyes smiled with pride. My beautiful sister was in the advertisement for Macy's.

It was an incredible feeling to be able to recall the things that made me happy. I only wished that time and circumstance had allowed us to do more things that brought us even closer together. I can't relive the days I spent watching air shows with my brother or laughing hysterically from the backseat of Troy's 1969 orange Z28 with two white stripes. He'd stolen a train horn and installed it on his car. When he blew it, the reactions were priceless. Meanwhile, I blasted people with a water weenie as he sped through town.

It's impossible to go back and tell my father I understood that he was in his own pain and to let go of it. And the tears my mother cried have long passed. Time and history cannot be altered, but what I *can* do is work towards showing my family how much I love them every day, the same way they love me.

———————

The bond I have with my family has become a vital part of me. I've learned that instead of hiding or running during our trials we should find strength and comfort in one another. When we do, whatever adversity we are faced with will pass and our relationship will be intact. I spent several years disconnected from everyone and had to rebuild everything. Now that my outlook on life is healthier, I won't squander any more time.

When I was in jail, the vision of the big oak tree had a powerful affect on me. It caused me to pray for my family with passion and love others even when I didn't have it for myself. But just as I was praying for them, they were praying for me.

We never know what secrets people carry or how they choose to handle them. And judgment is not the way to encourage or help someone overcome the adversity they're facing. Laughter doesn't mean there isn't pain behind it and success doesn't wash away problems. We will all face difficulties throughout our lives, but don't live without faith.

I believed the choices I made should have cost me my life. Regardless of my own attempts, they didn't. Death wasn't a part of the plan God had for me at that particular stage in my life. He wanted me to experience life the way it was destined. Learning to draw from the many lessons I had, helped me to progress in a healthy manner. In order to make that happen, I had to leave the pain behind. God gave me the tools to craft a better life a long time ago, but I never used them or activated the strength inside of me until the day of my spiritual awakening. It is because of God's grace and mercy that I am able to appreciate life and experience it on my feet with a heart full of joy.

It took years for me to understand the reason behind *the fall,* but it was simple. The pain I carried was heavier than my spirit could handle. I was in a fragile state as a kid and that weakness filtered into my adult life. Sometimes it's necessary to fall in order to learn how to fight. Rather than letting go and giving up, seek healthier alternatives. Life will continue to hurl inevitable challenges at each of us and we must be prepared to catch them. If we don't, and it knocks us down, get up as quickly as possible.

The Waves

You will feel it resonate inside of you with unexplainable power. Although you may not understand it, if you have faith–true faith, you will trust it because it's your gift from God warning you, teaching you, or saving you from yourself. Trust your intuition.

–Marala Scott

Serenity Prayer

Serenity Prayer

God grant me the Serienty
to accept the things I cannot change,
Courage to change the things I can
And the Wisdom to know the difference.

The Fall

Pride goes before destruction, a haughty spirit before
a fall. Proverbs 16:18 (NIV)

About the Author

Todd James Myers is an Author, Motivational Speaker, and Actor that inspires others to achieve their dreams through passion and faith. He is a father of four that resides in Northern California and spends his free time celebrating the gift of life. For more information, visit www.ToddJamesMyers.com.

Marala Scott is a Bestselling Author, Ghostwriter, Motivational Speaker, and Oprah's Ambassador of Hope who shares powerful words with uplifting messages wherever she goes. Marala was the consultant on *The Fall*, and is the author of *Intuition*, *In Our House, Surrounded By Inspiration*, and more. To learn about Marala, visit www.MaralaScott.com.